One in the GOSPEL

SECOND EDITION

One in the GOSPEL

The Formula of Concord for Our Day

FRIEDEMANN HEBART

OPENBOOK PUBLISHERS

A Study Guide for use with this book is available for purchase on disk from Openbook Publishers.

Cover design by Graeme Cogdell Imagart Pty Ltd

First edition published 1979
by Lutheran Publishing House (now Openbook Publishers)

First printing (second edition) January 2000
Third edition January 2005
08 07 06 05   10 9 8 7 6 5 4 3

National Library of Australia
Cataloguing-in-Publication data

Hebart, Friedemann, 1939-.
One in the gospel : the Formula of Concord for our day.

ISBN 0 85910 906 2.

Formula Concordiae. 2. Lutheran Church – Catechisms – English. I. Title.

238.41

Typeset by Openbook Publishers in 10pt Stone Sans

Printed and published by
Openbook Publishers
205 Halifax Street
Adelaide, South Australia 5000

Preface to the second edition

The background to this book was originally a series of articles I wrote twenty years ago to commemorate the 400th anniversary of the *Formula of Concord,* one of the lesser-known confessional writings of the Lutheran church. Subsequently, these articles appeared in amended form as a book. My chief intention was not to provide a commentary on the various theological controversies preceding the *Formula of Concord* and on the solutions which it provided. I was really more interested in trying to let the *Formula* speak to some of the basic questions and problems which people have with Christian faith as such. Of course, there have been considerable economic, social, political and technological changes since this book first appeared. Some of the references in the original edition are now outdated, and other revisions have become necessary. But I have tried to retain as much of the basic approach, style and content of the original edition as possible, since I don't think that the really important questions have altered much: What are we here for? Where are we heading? Is there a God who cares? What is expected of me?

In attempting to answer these and similar questions, I was guided not only by the *Formula of Concord* but also by the writings of Martin Luther. The fact that the writers of the *Formula of Concord* themselves referred to Luther as 'this highly enlightened man' and repeatedly quoted him as a decisive authority still seems to me sufficient justification for reading the Formula through Luther's spectacles. At any rate, the combination of the two seems to have been helpful over the years in answering some of the questions on the Christian faith raised by people today—and the whole process of understanding was greatly advanced by the excellent study guide prepared by the Rev David Strelan for the first edition, now carefully revised by the Rev John Pfitzner. Special thanks are also due to the latter for facilitating the publishing process in spite of the tyranny of distance.

Most scriptural quotations are from *The Holy Bible,* New Revised Standard Version (NRSV), copyright © 1989, by the Division of Christian Education of the National Council of the Churches of Christ in the USA. Other scriptural quotations are from the *Good News Bible: Today's English Version* (TEV), published by The Bible Societies/HarperCollins Publishers Ltd., UK, © American Bible Society, 1966, 1971, 1976, 1992; second edition 1994. *The Book of Concord,* tr and ed by Theodore G. Tappert, Muhlenberg Press, Philadelphia, 1959, supplied all quotations from the *Formula of Concord.* Page references to this work throughout the book are indicated in brackets after each quotation. (It will be observed that this work does not employ inclusive language.) Most quotations from the writings of Martin Luther are taken from *Luther's Works,* the American edition published conjointly by Concordia Publishing House, St. Louis, and Fortress Press, Philadelphia, 1955–1986. Some quotations I have translated directly from *D. Martin Luthers Werke,* Böhlau, Weimar, 1883 – , and these are indicated in the book by *WA.* References to *Luther's Large Catechism* are from my translation, © Lutheran Publishing House, Adelaide, 1983; and to *Luther's Small Catechism* from the translation published by Openbook Publishers, Adelaide, © 1996. Bibliographical references to other works quoted will be found at the back of the book; in the case of frequently quoted works, the page references are indicated in brackets in the text at the appropriate point.

Friedemann Hebart
Bayreuth, Germany
All Saints' Day, November 1999

Contents

Chapter 1. Discovering Our Identity	9
Chapter 2. Dialogue with the Gospel	15
Chapter 3. We Are Beggars—Is It True?	21
Chapter 4. How Do I Find Faith?	28
Chapter 5. No Strings Attached!	34
Chapter 6. Fruit on a Good Tree	43
Chapter 7. Sinners and Saints	49
Chapter 8. For Christ's Sake, Yes!	57
Chapter 9. Jesus Only	64
Chapter 10. Blueprint for Action	73
Chapter 11. Louder Than Words	86
Chapter 12. And There's No Other God	96
Chapter 13. Happy Ending?	108
Chapter 14. Free—to Serve the Gospel	116
Chapter 15. Chosen!	127
Chapter 16. Is God Choosy?	138
Chapter 17. Our Lutheran Identity	151
References	163

CHAPTER 1

Discovering Our Identity

The church records in my parish go back to the year 1602—an unbroken list of births, marriages and deaths for nearly four hundred years. Every week someone is to be found in the office poring over one of the old leather-bound volumes, trying to decipher the ancient handwriting and discover more about his or her ancestors.

Appreciating one's heritage

People are fascinated by their ancestors and usually proud of their heritage. Perhaps they go to such lengths to discover their roots because they hope to understand more about themselves.

The same is true of a country. It is only in the last decade or two that Australia has begun to develop its own national identity. For a long time we did not bother much about our heritage. But that has changed. We are now interested in the way people lived a century or more ago. Old buildings have been restored, and efforts have been made to preserve the original streetscapes of whole towns. If a country neglects its history and traditions, it loses its identity.

In all areas of life it seems to be important to us as human beings to know something of our background. Anyone who compares St Matthew's Gospel with the other gospels will be surprised that he starts such an exciting story with such a dull list of Jesus' ancestors. But what St Matthew is saying is that the list of ancestors must come first, if we want to understand and appreciate Jesus' identity. Jesus Christ is the climax and culmination of God's acts in a long period of history which started with Abraham. If we do not know that, we will have difficulty in grasping who Jesus is and why he came.

The church's identity

In the same way, the identity of a church is very much bound up with its history and background. People who are attracted to the life and worship, preaching and teaching of the Lutheran church and decide to take instruction before joining are usually most eager to find out something of the history and background of the Lutheran church beforehand. Why? Perhaps because they feel instinctively that part of what it means to be a Lutheran is to share in the history of God's acts in and with this church over the centuries. Our identity as Lutherans is something that comes down to us through our history and the heritage we receive.

Ignoring tradition

Strangely, one often finds that it is the 'new' Lutherans who are most interested in the heritage and traditions of the Lutheran church. On the whole, those of us who grew up as Lutherans take our background rather much for granted. We may not even know very much about it, apart from what we hear in an occasional sermon. In fact, we can even make a point of ignoring it.

One of the classic signs of immaturity is when young people think they cannot learn much of value from their parents' knowledge or experience. Theological immaturity is worse. It says that the past insights and experience of the church are irrelevant or meaningless to our secularised society today. For example, it has been claimed that Luther's question 'How can I find a gracious God?' is a question which was only raised by people in the Middle Ages, who were afraid of punishment and hellfire. The modern person's question is said to be quite different: 'Is there a God? How can I know God?'

But can we really say that the question of God's grace and goodness is irrelevant today? Aren't the modern questions 'How do I find happiness? How can suffering and misery in the world be removed? Who can help me understand the real meaning of life?' related to Luther's question of nearly five hundred years ago? The leaders of the Reformation lived so closely to the Bible that many of their writings are as up to date as the Bible itself.

Christians who dismiss their heritage are usually Christians without any real identity. They have no solid roots and are easily influenced by every new idea that comes along. You have to know where you come from in order to know where you are going.

Adoring tradition

Another way of losing our identity is to preserve our Lutheran heritage and revere it from a distance without using and applying it. Traditions are like a bank balance. Imagine that you inherited a hundred thousand dollars from your grandparents. You wouldn't dream of saying, 'That money was earned fifty years ago. It would be a shame to use it. I will have it framed as a memorial to my grandparents.' It would be short-sighted not to use inherited money as a basis for new investments today. Money that is not put to use is no more than a figure on a piece of paper.

The same is true of our Lutheran heritage. 'Pure doctrine' or 'divine truth' is not a quality you can 'have' or possess. It is something which—by the grace of God!—you may rediscover if you live close to the gospel and the heritage of the past. To be faithful to the Reformation and to discover one's identity as a Lutheran means to live in it, putting it to good effect.

There is a danger that we see the Reformation as something which happened once and is not repeated. But the word 'reformation' means renewal, and that means our heritage from the Reformation is never a quality we possess once and for all. It can be taken away from us 'and given to a people who will produce the proper fruits' (Matt 21:43 TEV). Individuals or even a church may subscribe officially to all the right teachings, celebrate anniversaries and the glorious memory of the church's great thinkers and teachers—and yet be in dire need of repentance and renewal. Our responsibility is not merely to preserve our past heritage, the way one might preserve an old building without living in it. Our duty is to allow the past to speak to us today and challenge us. We are to capitalise on the great treasure entrusted to our forbears and apply it to our own questions, hopes and fears.

The Formula of Concord

Therefore, to discover our identity as Lutherans involves two things. First, we must be prepared to find out all we can about our heritage. Secondly, we must ask what it means for us today.

One of the lesser-known pieces of our heritage and identity as Lutherans is the last and longest of the Lutheran confessional writings, called the *Formula of Concord.* Much of what we are as Lutherans has been influenced by this document, which the majority of Lutherans subscribed to between 1577 and 1580. In the chapters which follow we will try to discover what the *Formula of Concord* has to say to us today. We will allow it to challenge us, and we will see how so many of our deepest questions are answered by this 400-year-old document.

What is the *Formula of Concord*?

The *Formula of Concord* is a statement of agreement reached between various groups and individuals who were involved in disputes over the correct understanding of the gospel and the principles of the Lutheran Reformation. It is a long statement, divided into twelve chapters or articles which deal with the disputed points. Why did these disputes come about?

As long as Luther was alive he was the acknowledged authority on all matters of dispute. When he died in 1546, it seemed obvious at first that the mantle of leadership should fall on Luther's friend and right-hand man, Philip Melanchthon. He was as brilliant as he was modest, had been admitted to the University of Heidelberg at the tender age of thirteen, was professor of Greek at Wittenberg University at twenty-one, and had written the basic confession of the Lutheran church in 1530, the *Augsburg Confession*.

Luther and Melanchthon

What a contrast between these two leaders of the Reformation! Luther is dramatic and forceful; Melanchthon is shy and retiring. Luther is a practical person, concerned for the faith of ordinary people; Melanchthon is the born university teacher. Luther regards faith as the commitment of heart and life to God; for Melanchthon, faith is also a matter of the head and involves our intellectual agreement with information we receive about God. Luther is gruff and uncompromising where the truth is involved; Melanchthon is restrained and conciliatory.

While Luther was alive these tensions remained hidden. After his death, the strict Lutherans came to be increasingly suspicious of Philip Melanchthon and his followers. The 'Philippists', as they were called, felt that people were not quite as bad and helpless in God's sight as Luther had suggested. Statements like that were bound to irritate the strict Lutherans. In other ways, too, the Philippists showed that they were keen on compromise for the sake of unity with other Christians, such as Calvinists and Roman Catholics.

Unity or truth?

The unity of the churches is, of course, an important matter. Didn't Luther himself make it quite clear that the last thing he had wanted was a split in the church? And even after he was thrown out of the Roman church, didn't he admonish his followers in 1522 not to call themselves Lutherans but Christians? It is Christ who died for them, not Luther (*Luther's Works* 45,70f; 36,265)!

But truth is important too. Are people entirely dependent on God's mercy or not? Can I be sure that God has accepted me, or is there always an element of uncertainty? These questions, which were bandied back and forth between 'Lutherans' and 'Philippists' and were finally dealt with in the *Formula of Concord*, are matters of life and death. Truth is vital here. Unity or truth—that was one of the questions at stake.

Controversial questions resolved

One dispute led to another. Let us summarise just one or two in modern terms:

- When I go to holy communion, does Christ's forgiveness through his body and blood depend on how earnestly I confess my guilt and failings?
- If people with an alcohol or drug problem wish to join the church, should they be accepted before or only after they have licked the problem?
- When we see church members do something which is obviously wrong, should we 'throw the book at them' or quietly try to win them over by showing them what God has done for them?
- Among some non-Christians, the church today has a reputation of having a 'holier-than-thou' attitude and of being 'elitist'. Is it the church's duty to be a kind of guardian of morals and lay down the law when necessary?
- What is the use of the kind of Christianity where people *say* they believe, but their faith makes no apparent difference to their lives?
- Are you only half a Christian because you have questions and even doubts and cannot join in the enthusiasm of some of your friends?

These are only a few of the kinds of questions which the *Formula of Concord* helps us to answer.

It took years of struggle before unity was reached in the Lutheran church in 1577. The person who deserves acclaim for his patience and persistence was Jacob Andreae, a winning personality, deep thinker and fluent speaker. He regarded the unity of the church as his life's work, but he wanted to see the truth maintained as well. After many drafts, corrections, discussions and conferences involving many of the leading theologians of the time, the *Formula of Concord* was finally completed in May 1577.

The *Formula of Concord* was not a triumph for either of the disputing parties. It was an agreement based on the truth of the gospel, and it was written in a spirit of love, not anger. A total of eighty-six states or cities and 8188 pastors and teachers accepted it between 1577 and 1580. The majority of Lutherans had discovered their identity. Will we discover ours?

CHAPTER 2

Dialogue with the Gospel

It used to be quite common to say to one's children, 'Little children should be seen and not heard'. Today we have come to understand that children are usually more secure, alert and balanced when they grow up in normal and lively contact with the world around them. If they are encouraged to question, respond and interact in their own way, there are likely to be less problems with them than with children whose parents' main interest is to keep them quiet. Human beings, even the smallest of them, need interaction with other human beings in order to become normal, integrated individuals. In other words, they need to be involved in a dialogue where they hear and respond.

Monologue or dialogue?

That applies to adults too. We have all had the experience at a party where someone 'holds the floor'.We soon get restless and bored. We go to parties to meet other people and to get to know them better. But it is impossible to get to know a person when all the conversation is one-sided. We may get information about something, but there is no real contact with the person.

That is the difference between a monologue and a dialogue. In a monologue one person speaks and the other listens. There is no real communication, and a relationship between them cannot develop. You go to a talk to hear what a person has to say on a particular subject. You do not expect to get involved with the person giving the talk.

On the other hand, in a dialogue you are fully involved. You not only listen, you also respond. There is interaction. You share not only your ideas and experiences but also something of yourself. Real understanding and growth take place in me when I am completely involved in a dialogue with another person.

God involves us in a dialogue

Why is dialogue so important? Because we are made that way. From the very beginning we were created as people who can not only listen but also respond. We are made to be God's partners, to listen to God speaking to us and to respond as partners should. God speaks and acts and gives us the privilege of speaking and acting in return.

God does not speak to us in a monologue. God's word is not like a lecture, full of interesting information about what God or the world are like. God is trying to win us, not merely inform us. That is why not merely our minds and intellects are addressed. Instead God reaches out to make contact with us as people. When we listen to a sermon explaining a section of God's word in the Bible, on the surface it may seem to be a monologue. Actually it is *the beginning of a dialogue between God and us.* We are drawn into a relationship with God and we are challenged to react, to respond, to be part of God's life.

But often we understand God's word as though it were a monologue, a kind of textbook of teachings about God. And then we think that to be a Christian means to know certain facts about God and to agree to them. Rather, the Bible is God's dialogue with us. It is God reaching out to us.

Jesus Christ—God's personal word

In fact, God is so eager to enter into a personal dialogue with us that he joins us at our level. This is what St John means when he writes, 'The Word became flesh and lived among us' (John 1:14). Jesus does not just give us some new information *about* God. He comes and *is* God. In him God reaches out to make contact with us and makes it possible for us to respond by reaching out to make contact with him. This is why Jesus is called God's Word. And this is also why the Bible is called God's word, because in it God's personal dialogue with us human beings continues. In every word, God reaches out to us, wants to involve us, seeks our response. No wonder that this word of God is the only authority for what is preached and taught in the church!

Do we need confessions?

Now, anyone who glances at the *Formula of Concord* (in the collection of the Lutheran confessional writings of the sixteenth century known as the *Book of Concord*) will immediately be struck by the fact that it seems so different from the Bible. It looks very much like a collection of teachings *about* God and *about* theological questions. What business have we looking for our identity and heritage as Christians and Lutherans in that document? Isn't the word of God the only authority in the church? What use is a statement of beliefs more than four hundred years old? In other words, why do we need creeds and confessions when we have God's own word speaking to us? The *Formula of Concord* itself takes those questions seriously in its introduction. What is its answer?

When God speaks, the *Formula of Concord* points out, we always have to listen. When a pastor preaches on Sunday, when a Christian explains to a friend how God shares himself with us to the point of death in order to win our friendship and give us a share in his life, or when a person suddenly decides to let God in on a selfish marriage, they all have to listen first not to their own ideas but to God's side of the dialogue. The authority for everything we do as Christians, from the message we preach to the way we treat other people, must be the message Jesus preached and the way he treated other people, as described in God's word.

> We pledge ourselves to the prophetic and apostolic writings of the Old and New Testaments as the pure and clear fountain of Israel, which is the only true norm according to which all teachers and teachings are to be judged and evaluated. (pp 503,504)
>
> We believe, teach, and confess that the prophetic and apostolic writings of the Old and New Testaments are the only rule and norm. (p 464)

That is the answer of the *Formula of Concord.*

Our part in the dialogue

Do we then need creeds and confessions? Aren't they human words? Can they have authority?

Yes, they are human words. But we should remember that God always looks for a dialogue. Every word, every act of God looks for our *response.* People discover that God is speaking to them personally. They realise that God simply loves them—and not because they have turned over a new leaf or because they try to live fairly decent lives. They discover that Jesus' death on a cross is for them. They are overwhelmed. And they begin to respond to God's speaking.

Now at last a real dialogue begins. Communication develops between God and people. The friendship deepens. More and more people begin to express what they have discovered. Perhaps they cry out, 'Jesus is Lord' (Rom 10:9; Phil 2:11)—that is a confession of faith! Or they praise God—which is really the same thing (Matt 15:31; Luke 17:15). Or they fall down in wonder before Christ, 'the Son of the living God' (Matt 16:16). But the dialogue is catching on, the response to God's speaking is beginning, and more and more prayers and praises begin to rise up in the worship and confessions of the church:

The glorious company of the apostles praise you.
The noble fellowship of the prophets praise you.
The white-robed army of martyrs praise you.
Throughout the world the holy Church acknowledges you,
the Father of infinite majesty,
your adorable, true and only Son,
also the Holy Spirit, the Counsellor. (*Order of Matins*)

That is praise and confession and response and dialogue all in one. And that is the most fitting answer that human beings can give when God makes contact with them.

The writers of the *Formula of Concord* knew that. Why else would they have gone to such lengths to confirm the 'pure doctrine of the Word of God' (p 503)? The scriptures and the confessions together are God and human beings involved in a dialogue. God speaks, and we answer by confessing the marvellous things God has done.

Expressing our faith

Perhaps we are now beginning to understand why we have creeds and confessions which state what we believe. God involves us in a dialogue. God seeks our response. When we confess what we believe, to God and to the world, it is a response of our faith. In the same way each Sunday at worship the Bible readings and our confession of the creed are a dialogue between God and ourselves.

The *Formula of Concord* is therefore not an abstract statement of definitions about various questions which were in dispute among Lutheran theologians in the middle of the sixteenth century. It is an expression of faith, a response to the gospel, a dialogue with the gospel. The church's creeds and confessions are not definitions of what you *have* to believe as a Christian. They are a statement of what a Christian who is in a living relationship and dialogue with Jesus Christ in his word *does* believe. Lutherans do not believe that acceptance by God comes from having correct teachings. For example, you do not necessarily have faith when you can make the correct statement, 'I believe that the world was created by God'. But you do have faith when you can respond to God's act of creation by confessing, 'I believe that God has created *me' (Luther's Small Catechism,* Apostles' Creed, p 11)! Then *you* are in a dialogue with God; *you* are involved. The church's confessions help us to express that faith.

However, if what is being taught is wrong or misleading, the expression of faith and the response become dimmed. If the gospel is misunderstood, the dialogue with God is interrupted. For example, if I believed that Jesus was nothing more than a good man who gave us a magnificent example of self-sacrificing love, that would jeopardise my dialogue with God. For I could no longer be certain that God is my friend who came to share my life and my lot. God would be more like a distant, unapproachable being, whose mysterious ways I would have to live in fear of—or whom I would have to try to disregard. Therefore, it is important that we have confessions as 'witnesses and expositions of the faith', 'as witnesses to the truth' (pp 465,506).

Falsifying God's speaking

The church preaches, administers sacraments and makes decisions in a constantly changing world. Questions have to be answered and problems confronted which have perhaps never faced the church before and are not dealt with specifically in the Bible. How will the church know whether it is still proclaiming God's words and actions in accordance with God's speaking in the Bible? The church and its members are often in danger of falsifying God's speaking.

Here is just one example of the kind of issue that can arise. One well-known book on the Christian family tells us that to spare the rod is to spoil the child and quotes Proverbs 13:24 and 22:15 to prove it. Another book shows that the starting point of the Christian life is forgiveness and that the law of God and its threats do not remove sin. Who is right? How are we to act as Christian parents? What is God saying to us here? What is our correct response to God when he reaches out to us? Law or gospel? Punishment or forgiveness? Or both?

Of course, the Lutheran Confessions do not answer specific questions like these. But they do help us to understand the deeper intention of God's word. They help to clarify the main themes.

They explain the meaning of Scripture—and take a stand against those who digress from Scripture and whose dialogue with God is confused, unclear, misleading, or downright false. If we are going to praise God, let's do it properly!

Starting on a dialogue

The *Formula of Concord* wants to start us on a dialogue with God and his word. If it helps you to understand God's speaking to you and helps you to respond confidently, honestly, and joyfully, you will be on the way to discovering the inner secret of the Bible: God's dialogue with us.

C H A P T E R 3

We Are Beggars—Is It True?

It is a great event in a family's life when a baby is born. Relatives gather around the infant, vying with one another to discover whose looks the baby has inherited. They wouldn't dream of thinking that babies are personally responsible for their looks.

And as the child grows up and shows an interest in music, its grandmother may proudly proclaim that it has 'inherited' her musical talent. That is part of the child's heredity. It is not responsible for the gifts it has received.

We know today that a large part of our make-up depends on what we inherit from our parents and on our background. Of course, we often use the same argument as an excuse to explain why we lost our temper, or why our tongue got the better of us. Once I was called on to mediate in a bitter family squabble. Only after some time did one member of the family admit he had started the whole affair. But he immediately added, 'It's not really my fault. It's due to the hard life I've had. I can't change the way I am. The others ought to make allowances for me.' The man refused to admit he was morally responsible. He was 'passing the buck'.

'Passing the buck'

We are real experts at 'passing the buck' and making excuses for what we are. If I come home from a hard day at the office and am irritable with my wife, am I really responsible? Aren't my 'nerves' or my 'tiredness' responsible? Or are teenage drug addicts really responsible for what they are and the way they act, when we hear that they are often products of broken homes or have felt rejected at home? Surely the responsibility lies with their background or with their parents—or even with the society in which their parents were raised. People can't help what they are. Or can they?

Are we helpless victims?

We all sense that there is something terribly wrong with our world. There are the rifts in our families, social unrest, political strife, international and racial tensions. There is hideous brutality. The poor envy the rich and the rich exploit the poor. We are rapidly turning the planet Earth into a wasteland and have successfully torn vast holes in the mantle of ozone protecting us from the ravages of the sun. Can we be held personally responsible for all that? Aren't we born into a corrupt world? Isn't all the evil that people do part of our destiny as human beings, ever since Adam fell (Gen 3)? Aren't we helpless victims of Adam's sin?

The *Formula of Concord* in its Article I on *Original Sin* reminds us that the human being suffers from

> a deep, wicked, abominable, bottomless, inscrutable, and inexpressible corruption of his entire nature in all its powers,

as a result of which,

> since the Fall man inherits an inborn wicked stamp,

which he receives

> because of the disobedience of Adam and Eve. (p 510)

Hard words! But if we are born into that kind of world, what chance do we have? Can we hold ourselves responsible? Can't we 'pass the buck' to Adam?

'You are the man!'

It is certainly true that I inherit certain tendencies (such as my aggression) and certain values from my parents and ancestors. They are indeed part of my destiny.

But that doesn't mean I can 'pass the buck'. The *Formula of Concord* makes it clear that I am and remain guilty. How are we to understand that?

During World War II, Albert Einstein, a passionate pacifist, wrote a letter to President Roosevelt in which he pointed out what might happen if a maniac like Hitler were in control of atomic power. This warning was heeded, and work on the atomic bomb was speeded up. After the tragedy of Hiroshima in 1945 a woman said to Einstein, 'You were the first to press the button'. Einstein did not reply. He was dead-set against this terrible course of events; but it was his own research that set the avalanche of events moving. Although he could have 'passed the buck' and blamed the evil in the world, he knew he was responsible.

Whenever I am tempted, therefore, to disclaim responsibility for human corruption and evil, the *Formula of Concord* reminds me of Nathan's cry to David, 'You are the man!' (2 Sam 12:7). I cannot blame Adam and the fall for what *I am.* I am not simply a computer with a processor for a soul, carrying out the commands programmed into me. I actually *do* those evil things I know to be wrong (Rom 7:19). I have no alibi. The story of Adam and Eve is meant to show us what *all* human beings are like.

The question of responsibility

Of course, if sin were only a matter of individual actions, I could still excuse myself. And that is the real trouble. We like to think that sin is merely some evil thought, word or act by which we break one of God's rules. Thus, the more of God's rules you break, the bigger sinner you are. I suppose with a lot of effort and education we might remove some of our failings. I *need not* speed across the intersection as the light turns red and endanger a pedestrian's life; I *can* make an effort to deal with the attractive woman in the office with respect, and not merely as a prospective conquest to be made. But that doesn't mean I am no longer a sinner.

Sin is a radical break with God

The teaching of the Lutheran Confessions on original sin is very realistic. It says: Sin is not just what I do, it is what I am. Sin is more than evil deeds, and we cannot remove evil in the world by suppressing evil acts. If your daughter takes ten dollars from your wallet and you punish her, she may not steal again. But that doesn't mean that you have got rid of the underlying reason why your daughter took the money. The underlying reason for my wrong actions is that I am a 'slave to sin' (John 8:34). I regularly do wrong things because my basic attitude to God, to myself and to others is wrong. I trust myself instead of God and am indifferent towards other people. Sin is deeper than my failings. It is a radical break with God that we are all guilty of. From our birth we live on our own and for ourselves. We are, as the *Formula of Concord* puts it, 'by nature diametrically opposed to God and his highest commands' (p 510). For instance, a newborn child does not seem to do wrong. But for all that, it is 'curved in on itself' from the very start, as Luther never tired of saying. It is not naturally directed towards God, as parents soon discover! By nature we *are* selfish, we *are* greedy, we *are* adulterers, we *are* killers, whether we put it into practice or not. Have you ever had such aggressive feelings that you could have done someone real harm? Since we all *are* this way, there are really no greater or lesser sinners in God's sight. In God's sight I am no better than any of those characters whose horrible deeds blot the pages of history books.

Bad trees bear bad fruit

This means that sin is part of each person's make-up, no matter how 'good' or 'bad' that person may appear to us. The *Formula of Concord* makes that quite clear:

> Original sin is not a sin which man commits; it inheres in the nature, substance, and essence of man in such a way that even if no evil thought would ever arise in the heart of corrupted man, no idle word were spoken, or no wicked act or deed took place, nevertheless man's nature is corrupted through original sin. (p 468)

That is Jesus' own teaching, too: there is bad fruit on a tree because the tree is bad (Matt 7:17,18; 12:33–35; see also John 3:6). So Luther can even say: 'We constantly sin while doing good' (*Luther's Works* 31,61). No pastor or Christian counsellor would ever claim to *remove sin* when helping a couple to be reconciled.

Equality before God

If we accept that our whole system is infected with this 'spiritual leprosy' *(Book of Concord,* p 509), we will begin to see others with new eyes.

When facing a conflict in our families or at work we will realise that other people's sin arises from the same 'root and source' (p 508) as our own. We need not pretend to be better than they are. *'All of us* . . . are children of wrath by nature' (p 510, emphasis mine); we all equally deserve God's punishment. We will be less ready to criticise and preach at others when we know that.

The same is true in industrial relations. We will not be so quick to blame increased unemployment on workers who are not prepared to take lower wages, or on employers who are not prepared to sacrifice maximum profits. Rather, we will see the root problem in the basic self-centredness of all people and the greed of 'every one of us' (p 510). If we were not 'diametrically opposed to God' (p 510) in the first place, we would not be constantly seeking our own advantage at the expense of others.

Those of us who attend church services regularly and see ourselves as clean-living, upright members of society need to read the *Formula of Concord* on original sin more than anyone else. Why is it that our churches so often attract only a certain 'type' of person? Is it because all those people 'on the edge of society', as we so nicely put it, sense that we feel morally superior to them and see us as 'elitist'? The *Formula of Concord* reminds us that in God's sight all people are indeed equal—in sin.

Evidence of original sin

Original sin is not sin that can be recognised.

> This damage is so unspeakable that it may not be recognized by a rational process, but only from God's Word. (p 467)

If I always look at myself in a distorted mirror I can never know what I am really like. Only when God's word tells me of the lengths to which God goes to forgive me, by dying on the cross for me, can I begin to see how great my corruption is.

Qualifying for God's mercy

But why all this talk of sin? Are people really as evil as the *Formula of Concord* makes them out to be? Don't they achieve great and noble things? Aren't they capable of immense sacrifices? Wouldn't it be better to develop these powers?

The *Formula of Concord* takes issue with a Lutheran professor in Jena, Victorin Strigel, who took a view like this. He maintained that we are evil, but not thoroughly so; our spiritual powers are like a blot or stain; the Holy Spirit can take away this blot and bring out the deep goodness in us (see rejected doctrine No. 5, pp 511,512).

We often think along those lines. We are kind to animals; we pay our taxes; we stick to the speed limits; we do not willingly hurt anyone; we are good, clean-living people. True, the world is not as it should be, but—so we argue—in creation God gave us certain powers which can be of real, positive good for the world, and there's a good spark in each one of us. Why then should God be so angry with us?

The God of outsiders

The *Formula of Concord* rejects this view; human nature can do nothing but sin (p 512). The writers knew that people who see themselves with a 'good spark' will soon feel that they do not need God's grace and so will lock Christ out of their lives. Only when we realise that with all our powers we are 'dead indeed to that which is good' (p 519) will we know how much we need God's forgiveness every day. To deny or lessen sin is, as Luther points out, to 'cheapen Christ's grace and minimize God's mercy' *(Luther's Works* 32,240). God comes only to outsiders—those in utter disgrace. That is just what Jesus did (Mark 2:15–17). By stressing sin, the *Formula of Concord* is not out to give us an inferiority complex. Instead it confesses the most important of all miracles Jesus did: the miracle of God's forgiveness.

Are we created evil?

But if we are thorough sinners, are we created evil? That was the line taken by Strigel's opponent, the over-zealous Matthias Flacius. He was afraid that Strigel might be denying the power of God's loving mercy, and so he went to the other extreme: human beings are so evil that they have become transformed into the 'true and living image of the devil'. After the fall, said Flacius, every trace of a relationship with God was rubbed out.

Strigel protested. Surely Flacius was saying that God is the creator of sin. Don't we continue to live in a relationship with God even if that relationship is utterly wrong? Indeed, if our *created* nature as such is evil we really are no longer responsible for what we are and we can cheerfully excuse ourselves. God is responsible.

The *Formula of Concord* rejects Flacius's wrong teachings too (pp 512–515). If we were such monsters, Jesus would always remain a stranger to us. If we are no longer God's creatures, but the devil's, how could Jesus become one of us? He could not be my brother. How could he save us unless he took *our* nature?

> In the article of our redemption we have the mighty testimony of Scripture that God's Son assumed our nature, though without sin, so that in every respect he was made like us, his brethren, sin alone excepted (Heb 2:17). (pp 515,516)

Unworthy but not worthless

The *Formula of Concord* helps us to understand: no matter what I am, I cannot cut myself off from God. 'Even after the fall our nature is and remains a creature of God' (p 466). I am unworthy, but I am not worthless to God. I am always God's child even though everything in me resists him. The parable of the prodigal son tells us the same (Luke 15:11–24). I may let God go, but he doesn't let me go.

That is an important point for those who engage in evangelism or social work. No matter how low some people may sink in our sight, God has not broken off all contact with them. He continues to love them because he made them.

Each year we have a special opportunity before Easter to meditate on our Lord's suffering and death. If we allow the *Formula of Concord* to show us what our true colours are, we may begin to grasp something of the wonderful release and freedom and joy that Jesus' cross brings us. He was punished for what we are (2 Cor 5:21; Gal 3:13). We are *and remain* sinners—and yet we are accepted by God because of Good Friday.

Luther put it another way—his last written words: 'We are beggars, that is true' (*Luther's Works* 54,476).

C H A P T E R 4

How Do I Find Faith?

Millions of people now living in Australia or in the USA originally came from other countries. They will often tell you that as the train or boat left on the first leg of the journey, many looked back and waved to a father or mother whom they might never see again. At that moment they had an overwhelming sense of helplessness. They had chosen to go, had torn up their roots, and now it was too late to change their minds. They could not stop the train; they had to go on.

Our relationship to God is something like that. From the very moment of our birth we are helplessly caught in the 'train' of our selfish nature. We have chosen to go our own way apart from God, and now we find we cannot get off this 'train'. We are free only to keep on going. The *Formula of Concord* in its Article II on *Free Will* does not mince words:

> The natural free will is mighty and active only in the direction of that which is displeasing and contrary to God. (p 521)

The Spirit creates faith

Most people find this very hard to accept. One of today's most cherished beliefs is the notion that we are free to control our own destiny. It is said that people become Christians because they choose to do so. That means that the pastor's task is to make people *want* to believe of their own free will.

The *Formula of Concord* denies that. Quoting a host of biblical passages, it states:

> The free will by its own natural powers can do nothing for man's conversion, righteousness, peace, and salvation, cannot cooperate, and cannot obey, believe, and give assent when the Holy Spirit offers the grace of God and salvation through the Gospel. (p 524)

If a person comes to have faith in Christ, it is 'altogether and alone' the work of the Holy Spirit (p 526).

Doing our bit

Can we really accept that? If a friend gives me a birthday present, I can take it or leave it; surely that is also true of God's peace and salvation? If we cannot even accept God's offer of forgiveness and peace, then surely we can only become Christians against our will. This was the argument raised after Luther's death by the three theologians, Philip Melanchthon, John Pfeffinger, and Victorin Strigel. If it is not up to us whether we are Christians or not, we might very well ask why the Holy Spirit gives faith to some and seems to withhold it from others. It seems unfair. No, they said, we must do our bit. Certainly, the Holy Spirit is offered to us first by God's grace; but we have to accept him. The step of faith is up to us, they claimed. Otherwise, they said, we are no longer responsible for whether we believe in Christ or not.

A decision for Christ?

There is a movement in the churches which argues along these lines. Many Christians feel that people are free to 'get off the train' of their sinful nature and turn to God, once they have heard the message of his love. And so they make a passionate appeal to sinful people: 'Give yourself to Jesus! Invite him into your heart! Make a decision for Christ!' When the gospel has been preached, they argue, people must decide for themselves. They must put their lives into Jesus' hands. A book on charismatic Christianity once put it this way: 'You must take the first step'.

The *Formula of Concord* rejects this popular view of faith. How can a person who is imprisoned become free by making a decision? My first steps bring me slap up against the prison walls. Faith has to be given to me by the Holy Spirit.

'I cannot believe!'

But that really puts us on the spot! Time and again people say to me: 'Pastor, I would desperately like to believe. I hear the words of the gospel and I long for peace of mind and an end to my doubts. I search desperately for faith. I've wrestled with God. I've cried out to him again and again. Sometimes I think I believe, but the very next day I feel only emptiness and darkness. And then I don't even know whether there is a God. Apparently faith is something you either have or don't have. It has to be given to you. Well, it hasn't been given to me.'

There are people like that in every congregation. They genuinely want faith, but they cannot believe. They feel they are only half-Christians, or not even Christians at all. Others have had their faith shattered by a personal tragedy.

If it is the Holy Spirit who gives us faith, as the *Formula of Concord* states, we have no reason to feel superior to those who doubt and question. We have done nothing to deserve our faith. Rather, we should deal with doubts and questions in humility and love.

But what can people do to find faith, if faith depends 'altogether and alone' on the 'divine operation of the Holy Spirit' (p 526)?

The writers of the *Formula of Concord* take up this question. They are aware that

> despondent hearts may fall into grave anxiety and doubt, and wonder if God has really elected them and actually purposes through his Holy Spirit to work these gifts of his within them, since they feel no strong, ardent faith and cordial obedience but only weakness and anxiety and misery. (p 530)

First step: God's call

How, then, do I find faith? According to the *Formula of Concord,* the starting point is not anything *I* do but something that *God* does. It is not God's will to reject anybody.

That is why 'through his holy Word (when one hears it preached or reads it) and the sacraments (when they are used according to his Word)' (p 531), God's call goes out through the Holy Spirit, and he actually converts people.

> The preaching and the hearing of God's Word are the Holy Spirit's instrument in, with, and through which he wills to act efficaciously, to convert men to God, and to work in them both to will and to achieve. (p 531)

I do not 'invite Jesus into my heart'; I do not solve all my doubts and questions first. Even before I begin to grasp that I am a sinner, God's call goes out to me and tells me that I am accepted, I belong. As a hymn puts it:

Love that found me—wondrous thought!
Found me when I sought him not.
('Chief of sinners though I be')

Becoming a Christian and having faith is not the end-result of all my efforts to understand; it is a movement which starts with God through his word and through baptism. Naturally, as the *Formula of Concord* stresses, I must hear this message (p 531), and that may require effort and patience on my part. After all, I do have the freedom to 'go to church, listen to the sermon, or not listen to it' (p 531).

Second step: dare to ask

The second step of faith is a vital one, too. I must dare to ask Jesus for help. The well-known theologian and preacher Helmut Thielicke once spoke of the 'wallflowers on the border' of the New Testament. None of these 'wallflowers' has faith as we usually understand it. They seem to have very little idea about who Jesus really is. The woman with the haemorrhage (Mark 5:25–34) does not call him Son of God or Son of David. We are not told that she had listened to Jesus' message. She is not even interested in meeting Jesus personally. Apparently she has heard a rumour of his marvellous powers and so she creeps up from behind to get hold of his 'magic' for herself. Sheer superstition, we are tempted to say. You would expect Jesus to correct her wild ideas. Instead, he gives her more than she could ever have hoped for—and extols her faith!

What is this faith? Merely the fact that on the basis of a rumour *she dares to come to Jesus for help.* No more! But no less either!

'Spark of faith'

Or think of the distraught father of the epileptic boy (Mark 9:17–29). His cry, 'I believe; help my unbelief', is quite spontaneous. What does he believe? The text suggests he has some real doubts: '. . . but if you are able to do anything . . .' (v 22). That sounds very much as though he has not really understood who he is dealing with. And yet he has taken the greatest step of faith possible; he has dared to look to Jesus for help: 'Have pity on us and help us' (v 22). Isn't that cry already the 'spark of faith' which the Holy Spirit creates (p 531)? And doesn't Jesus himself say, 'Blessed are those who hunger and thirst for righteousness, for they will be filled' (Matt 5:6)?

Faith begins when I have reached the end of all *my* possibilities, stand there with empty hands—and look to Jesus for help. Then the biggest step of faith has already been taken.

God finds us

But isn't this a step of *our* free will if we cry out to Jesus for help?

St Augustine once wrote: 'We would not be able to seek God,

if he had not already found us'. The very fact that a person who doubts cries out to Jesus for help is a sign that the Holy Spirit is already at work in that person. It is the Holy Spirit who prompts the cry (Rom 8:26). That is why the desperate plea 'Lord, help me!' is already trust and faith. The *Formula of Concord* is very comforting when it quotes Philippians 2:13: 'For it is God at work in you, enabling you both to will and to work for his good pleasure', and comments:

> This appealing passage is of very great comfort to all devout Christians who perceive and discover a little spark and a longing for the grace of God and eternal salvation in their hearts. They know that God, who has kindled this beginning of true godliness in their heart, wills to continue to support them in their great weakness and to help them to remain in true faith until their end. (p 523)

Third step: certainty—not security

Of course, measured against the Lutheran Confessions, there may still be great gaps in your faith. But there is not one instance in the New Testament where Jesus leaves a person begging in vain—where he does not respond. A person who receives a tiny spark of faith from the Holy Spirit and turns to Jesus for help will look for more and more understanding of God's word in a lifetime process of growth. Continue to discover Christ! Go to church! Study the Bible! Don't give up! One day you *will discover* what it means to call Jesus the Son of God. God builds up slowly, in his own way.

That growth may be steady. It may have dark and barren periods. It may seem to you that you are making no progress at all. And there are varieties of faith. One person bubbles over with joy; another is quietly certain; another bores deeply and wants to understand everything; another is always searching and crying out to God—and is envious of the inner certainty of other Christians. But the Christian life is rarely a time of perfect security. According to Matthew 8:23–27, being a disciple means that Jesus can lead you into a terrible storm—and then simply go off to sleep. 'Press on!' says Luther on this text. 'Christ is with me in the boat; if I drown, he'll have to put up with it too!' (*WA* 49,334,335; see also Rom 8:35!).

Faith is like climbing a mountain. There are so many dark valleys, and only rarely do we get a clear, breathtaking view from the peak. Therefore,

> we ought to petition [God] . . . incessantly that by the . . . Spirit and grace, through daily exercise in reading his Word and putting it into practice, he would preserve faith and his heavenly gifts in us and strengthen us daily until our end. (p 523)

Perhaps God sometimes allows us to be a bundle of misery to remind us that our faith has no human support. Reason and feelings are dead, and we are forced to depend on God's Holy Spirit alone.

> The conflict and warfare of the flesh against the Spirit continues also in the elect and truly reborn. (p 534)

But we can have certainty, even if there is no guarantee of security. God in Christ won the victory over everything that can separate us from God. And through the Holy Spirit we are given a share in God's own life—long before we have found our way to him.

CHAPTER 5

No Strings Attached!

One of the biggest problems facing many western nations today is the fact that an increasing number of firms each year is going bankrupt or being forced to close down operations. Over the years, the prices of products have risen to meet growing costs and to foot increased wage bills. Meanwhile, in other parts of the world, employees work for long hours with few benefits so that goods can be produced cheaply, forcing the more expensive competitors off the international market. What is the solution to the problem? Firms with innovative products will survive. But what does a firm do which produces household goods or decorative articles? Some say we will need to take a new look at our wage structures if we are to remain competitive. Apart from the industrial unrest this would cause, the question is: If I work for someone haven't I a right to a fair and equitable reward? Where will it all end if we start upsetting the balance between pay and performance?

Rewards and punishment

The same principle applies in the world of law and justice. If you speed in a built-up area at 100 km/h you need not look surprised if you are stopped by the police and receive a stiff fine. You get what you deserve. Our world is based on a system of rewards for performance and punishments for misdemeanours. That is justice.

But what if *God* were to treat us as we really deserve? If it's true that we are 'by nature diametrically opposed to God and his highest commands', as the *Formula of Concord* states in Article I (p 510), then surely we can only expect our just deserts? God must refuse to have anything more to do with us—and that means eternal death and condemnation.

God says yes

That was the terrible problem the young Luther struggled with. Only after many years of inner turmoil did he discover the comforting teaching of the New Testament. The *Formula of*

Concord in Article III on *The Righteousness of Faith before God* joins in calling this teaching 'the chief article of the entire Christian doctrine' (p 540).

> We poor sinners are justified before God and saved solely by faith in Christ, so that Christ alone is our righteousness. (p 472)

In Romans 1:17 and 3:21–28, Luther read that we are simply accepted and acquitted by God, with no strings attached. We do *not* get what we deserve. The father accepts the lost son without ifs and buts and maybes (Luke 15:11–32). He doesn't put him on probation. He doesn't even forgive him on the condition that he turns over a new leaf afterwards. God simply says yes to us—as we are.

God accepts the ungodly

Understandably the *Formula of Concord* waxes enthusiastic about this discovery of the gospel:

> We believe, teach and confess . . . that a poor sinner is justified before God (that is, he is absolved and declared utterly free from all his sins, and from the verdict of well deserved damnation, and is adopted as a child of God and an heir of eternal life) without any merit or worthiness on our part, and without any preceding, present, or subsequent works, by sheer grace. (pp 540,541)

God does the impossible: he accepts the ungodly (Rom 4:5). It makes no difference whether you consider yourself an upright, decent and respected member of society or whether you are generally regarded as beyond help. In God's judgment you are equal in sin—and yet you are equally acquitted.

'For the sake of Christ's obedience'

Does that mean that God simply excuses and whitewashes us? Does he consider ungodliness harmless? No, it is not like that. In God's sight we are not right. The whole wonderful secret of his forgiveness is that Jesus Christ is right in God's sight. When Jesus died in full obedience to God's will for him, he put himself on the very spot where we ought to be. It was God's loving will that Jesus should die instead of us. He got what *we* deserve.

By dying on the cross, he had our bankrupt firm transferred to his own divine name. God, looking at Jesus, saw us in our sin and punished him in our place. And now when he looks at us he sees Jesus' innocent and obedient death, and so he accepts and forgives us. The *Formula of Concord* makes a point of stressing

> that a poor sinner is justified before God . . . by sheer grace, solely through the merit of the total obedience, the bitter passion, the death, and the resurrection of Christ, our Lord, whose obedience is reckoned to us as righteousness. (pp 540,541)

We are and remain people who turn away from God (p 543), and yet because of Christ's work for us we are simply treated as though we were perfect. We are accepted sinners.

Message of comfort

This is the central message of the gospel. It is an immense comfort to people who are frustrated and unhappy because they have a deep sense of guilt, to those who know they are not what they should be, and to those who are 'consumed in the hell-fire of life', as the German writer Hebbel once put it. They should be delighted to hear that God accepts them without strings attached.

We in the church should be spending much more time with the down-and-out, the wavering and the hopeless—those who are anxiously looking for someone to accept them as they are. They are the ones most likely to grasp this message of comfort.

Goodness doesn't count

By the same token, it is hard for respected members of the church and of society to accept the fact that they are forgiven without any conditions. Many people work hard at their lives. They try to avoid conflicts. They are honest in financial matters. They are not guilty of sexual promiscuity. They are deeply concerned about the trends in modern society. They make regular contributions to the disadvantaged. They may even be members of the church 'in good standing', work hard for the church and give up their time for church work. It is harder for such solid, upright people to realise that none of these qualities influences God in the least when he accepts them. After all, it must surely make a difference what kind of life you lead; it must be worth something, they argue.

The *Formula of Concord* stresses that *none* of this counts when it comes to God accepting us:

> God forgives us our sins purely by his grace, without any preceding, present, or subsequent work, merit, or worthiness, and reckons to us the

> righteousness of Christ's obedience, on account of which righteousness we are accepted by God into grace and are regarded as righteous. (p 473)

There are no conditions we can or must fulfil to be accepted by God. But the Formula's teaching on righteousness does make one big demand on us. It expects us to respond to God's loving acceptance in trust.

> The Holy Spirit offers these treasures to us in the promise of the Gospel, and faith is the only means whereby we can apprehend, accept, apply them to ourselves, and make them our own. (p 541)

Christ for us or in us?

Andreas Osiander, a passionate, energetic personality, did not like this kind of talk. He felt that we must surely *be* righteous before God can fully accept us. We have to be *made* into good people by God and not just regarded or *treated* as good people. On the basis of texts like Romans 8:9–11 and Ephesians 3:17 Osiander claimed that Christ actually comes to live in us, and that makes a *visible* difference to our lives. We are changed. And that is why God accepts us. Righteousness, said Osiander, is like a medication which makes a person well again. Christ lives in the believer, who then looks and feels better. How will you know that Christ is living in you? When you experience the improvement in your life! It is what you experience in yourself that is important, he claimed.

Osiander today

Unfortunately, this is still a widespread view in churches today. People like to believe that they are right with God because they see improvement in their lives. They say: You have to be a new person first before God can fully accept you. You have to show that you mean it. Perhaps you find that you do not always have a deep sense of faith. Or you have no real feelings of happiness and release. Or you discover that your pet sins are still getting the better of you. Too bad, these people say; it just goes to show that the Holy Spirit is not yet at work in you.

Others say: You can tell that God has accepted you by the holy life you lead. If you have an alcohol problem or some other sin, it is a clear sign that God is not yet living in you. You can become a Christian only after you have licked that problem, they claim.

Osiander is still very much alive, even in the Lutheran church. Some church members are still reluctant to attend holy communion, because they believe they must clean up their lives first, or at least *feel* genuinely that they are sinners before they can receive Christ's forgiveness through his body and blood. We like to make all kinds of conditions for God's justification and forgiveness in Christ.

Troubled consciences

Because of views like this, I venture to say that a very large number of Christians are unsure and troubled in their faith. Instead of looking to what God has done in Jesus Christ, they look into their own hearts, and naturally they do not find very much spirituality there to comfort them. For what if I discover that, having heard the gospel, I am still not living a holier life? What if I do not always *feel* despondent about my sin? Is that not a clear sign that I am not accepted by God?

Osiander soon found himself faced with a barrage of criticism, led by Joachim Moerlin and Philip Melanchthon. They pointed out that despairing, troubled people need the assurance that they *are* all right with God and that God accepts them without conditions.

For what happens when my faith wavers or falters? When I feel nothing? When a personal tragedy such as the loss of my life's partner or my child severely rocks my faith? What happens when I fight my bad temper or my gossiping tongue or my roving eye, and yet they get the better of me? What happens when I try to trust God with joy in my heart but again and again find myself timid, nervous and worried? How can I ever trust that I am really accepted by God when I see so little evidence of it in my life? Those are the tortuous questions Osiander's teaching raises. And who doesn't know them? If we follow Osiander, our Christian life must become an endless soul-searching and self-examination and a matter of fear and doubt.

God accepts us without conditions

The writers of the *Formula of Concord* follow the gospel here, and so they can offer great comfort. God justifies us without conditions. The message of the gospel does not say, 'If you do this…' or 'If you feel that…' It says, 'Your sins *are* forgiven' (Mark

2:5); 'You *all* are children of God' (Gal 3:26). So the *Formula of Concord* says (emphasis mine):

> . . . A poor sinner *is* justified before God . . . (p 540)
>
> . . . we *have* forgiveness of sins by grace . . . (p 541)
>
> . . . they [the believers] *are* regarded as holy and righteous through faith . . .

and adds

> even though, on account of their corrupted nature, they are still sinners and remain sinners until they die. (p 543)

God accepts us for Christ's sake—not for ours; and God's justification is not affected by our changing feelings and moods. We have to learn that God justifies the *ungodly* (Rom 4:5)—even the ones without feelings, deep devotion and a respectable life. God accepts us not because we are good Christians but despite the fact that we are not!

> In order to afford saddened consciences dependable and reliable comfort and to give due honor to the merit of Christ and the grace of God, Scripture teaches that the righteousness of faith before God consists solely in a gracious reconciliation or the forgiveness of sins . . . accordingly in justification before God faith trusts neither in contrition nor in love nor in other virtues, *but solely in Christ* and . . . in his perfect obedience with which he fulfilled the law of God in our stead and which is reckoned to the believers as righteousness. (p 544; see also pp 474,545)

Nothing could be clearer than that. What is important is not how we see ourselves but how God sees us!

Do we lick our problems first?

All this means there are no conditions *I* have to fulfil to receive God's forgiveness and love. There is a story told by a Christian writer which may shock us at first, but which expresses the deep comfort which the *Formula of Concord* gives us on the basis of texts such as Romans 1:17; 3:28; 5:5–8.

> One evening several years ago I was taking a friend out to dinner. We had eaten in a cafeteria when a good-looking young woman sauntered up to our table. I recognized the woman as a member of the large Sunday-school class I taught. We began to talk. After about 40 minutes she said almost wistfully,
>
> 'I really believe you've found hope in your faith, and I would honestly like to make this beginning commitment of my life to Christ . . . but I can't do it.'
>
> 'Why not?' I asked gently.

'Because I've got a personal problem that I can't seem to resolve.' She was biting her lips and looking down at a paper napkin she had folded into a small bulky square.

'But that's why Christianity is called "good news",' I said, coming on strong. 'We can't solve our basic hang-ups and separations. I can't promise to change anything. All I can do is to accept his love and grace.'

'But', and she hesitated . . . 'I don't feel acceptable until I whip this problem.'

'Listen, Susan, the old song doesn't say, "Just as I am when I whip my major problem". It says, "Just as I am without *one plea"*— one *promise,* one *guarantee*!'

She looked at me with the strangest dawning look of hope. 'Do you really believe that?' she said.

'I'd bet my life on it.'

She looked down at her hands for several minutes. 'All right,' she said, almost as a challenge, 'I'm committing adultery every Thursday night with a man who has a wife and several young children. And I *cannot* quit. Now can I come into your Christian family?'

I just looked at her. I certainly had not expected that. My first conditioned reaction as a Christian churchman would have been to think she is not ready for Christ.

Suddenly I realized how phoney we Christians are. Of course we *would* expect her to quit committing adultery. We don't mean 'Just as I am without one plea.' We actually mean, 'Just as I am when I *promise* implicitly to straighten up and quit my major sins.' And this girl had nailed me with her honesty. She knew she did not have the strength to quit her 'sinning'. And yet it was her weakness which had brought her toward Christ in the first place.

I thought about Jesus and what he would have done. Then I looked up at her, 'Of course, you can commit your life to Christ just as you are,' I smiled. 'He knows you want to quit seeing this man, and I don't know where else you can ever *hope* to find the security and strength to break up with him. So if you commit your life to Christ right now, then Thursday night, if you find you can't help meeting your friend, take Christ with you in your conscious mind through the whole evening. Ask him to give you the desire and the strength to break off the relationship.'

And she stepped across the stream and became a Christian.

(Keith Miller, *Habitation of Dragons*)

How hard it is for us to realise that the gospel promise has no strings attached! But the drug-addict, the wife-beater and every obvious sinner can take heart. For that is the gospel. And the church which really preaches the justification of the ungodly will always accept a person like that *first*; and then it will trust that the new believer will be helped by the power of the Holy Spirit to lick his or her problem.

Faith a condition?

But isn't faith a condition? Doesn't the *Formula of Concord* stress with St Paul how vital it is that we have faith, if God is to accept us (p 541)? Are there conditions after all?

We always forget that faith is a matter of taking hold of Christ long after he has found us and accepted us. Luther compared faith to a person who is drowning in a stream and catches hold of the branch of a tree for support (*Luther's Works* 12,262). Faith is the hand that reaches out for God's gift. It is not necessarily a feeling and it certainly is not a virtue (*Book of Concord*, p 541). We are not meant to search ourselves for feelings of trust. We are meant to look to Jesus Christ and what he has done for us. Faith, as Edmund Schlink once put it, is the 'astonished realization' that God reaches out to us. Nothing more! There are no strings attached.

Worthy participation in communion

This means that our worthy participation in holy communion never depends on how deeply we *feel* our sins, *feel* contrition, or on how much of the mess in our Christian life we have cleaned up. God wants to give us forgiveness in the sacrament; he does not expect or allow us to try to earn it. Worthy participation depends merely on whether we expect and hope to receive the benefits of Christ's death and resurrection. Anyone who denies that should read what Luther says! 'Dear fellow', he writes, 'you must not look at yourself, how worthy or unworthy you are, but at your need . . . of the grace of Christ . . . At least believe the Scripture, if you cannot trust your feelings' (*Luther's Works* 38,129,132).

The *Formula of Concord* says the same thing:

> Neither is contrition nor love nor any other virtue the means and instrument with and through which we could receive and accept the grace of God, the

merit of Christ, and the forgiveness of sins offered to us in the promise of the Gospel, but only faith. (p 544)

Sin meant to be cured, not cherished

Of course that does not mean 'that we may or should follow in the ways of sin, abide and continue therein without repentance, conversion, and improvement' (p 543). We should bear that in mind when we go to holy communion.

But an improvement of this kind is not a *condition* for us to receive Christ's true body and blood. All that is required is that we depend on God's forgiveness. There are no ifs and buts and maybes in the gospel. That is the truth which the *Formula of Concord* sees so clearly. There is merely the statement of God: guilty—and yet acquitted! If we go on our feelings or virtues we are insulting God. Instead we are to

. . . preserve the glory due to Christ . . . (p 545)

. . . give due honor to the merit of Christ and the grace of God . . . (p 544)

. . . give all glory to Christ alone. (p 474)

The heart of the gospel

The doctrine of justification on account of Christ through faith is the very heart of the gospel message. As C. F. Walther pointed out a long time ago, if we lose this message we lose everything in the Christian faith. It is the teaching by which the church stands or falls.

CHAPTER 6

Fruit on a Good Tree

Can you set a price on a person's love? Can you judge the extent of someone's care by the size of the presents you receive? Most of us would immediately answer, 'Of course not!'

One of the biggest lessons young couples in love have to learn is to measure each other's gifts—and actions—by their love for each other. To people who really love, a tiny flower or an encouraging word at the right time can mean more than a valuable ring or an expensive watch. It's not really the flower or the word which is valuable but the love which it expresses. You don't evaluate the flower given to you by your husband by going to the florist to find out what it cost. You accept it as a token of your husband's love.

A gift or an action has no value on its own. It depends on the reasons for which it is done and how it is seen through the eyes of love. Parents will value the 'worthless' little works which their children make for them in hours of painstaking effort more highly than the tasteful works of art in their home.

The person makes the deed good

The *Formula of Concord* in Article IV on *Good Works* claims that the Christian life is similar to that. People outside the Christian faith—and unfortunately quite a number within it—tend to evaluate good deeds by their size or value. But according to the *Formula of Concord*, what makes a deed good and valuable to God is the love and trust of the person behind it—and the eyes of love with which God accepts it:

> The good works of believers are pleasing and acceptable to God, even though they are still impure and imperfect . . . because the person is acceptable to God. (p 552)

Article IV of the *Formula of Concord* adds that if God regards us as good, 'for the sake of the Lord Jesus Christ through faith' (p 552), then what we do *is* good, if done through faith. As Luther puts it in his *Treatise on Good Works*, everything a person 'does in faith is well done in God's sight' (*Luther's Works* 44,26). He even said somewhere that if it were possible for me to commit adultery in faith (it isn't!), it would be a good deed! Faith always does good. Therefore the *Formula of Concord* quotes Luther's famous statement:

> Oh, faith is a living, busy, active, mighty thing, so that it is impossible for it not to be constantly doing what is good. Likewise, faith does not ask if good works are to be done, but before one can ask, faith has already done them and is constantly active. (pp 552,553; see also p 545)

'Splendid vices'

But the opposite is true too. Anything I do without faith is in God's sight worse than useless. St Augustine called all 'good' deeds done apart from faith 'splendid vices'. Quoting Matthew 7:18 ('A good tree cannot bear bad fruit, nor can a bad tree bear good fruit') and Romans 14:23 ('Whatever does not proceed from faith is sin'), the *Formula of Concord* states that 'works which . . . do not flow from true faith . . . are sinful' (p 552). You can never judge by the deed; it is the person behind it that counts.

The fruit depends on the tree

This means that much of what people usually regard as good may not be good at all. Our regular church attendance, our deep concern for peace and justice in the world, our great generosity for church or social work may be an expression of faith. Then it is good. But it may be done for what we get out of it. Then it is worthless in God's sight. The tiniest word of kindness, spoken spontaneously in faith and obedience to God, is 'pleasing and acceptable' to him (p 552). Love can feed the hungry—but so can pride. Love for God can make me work conscientiously at my job—but so can ambition. We should remember this when we are tempted to evaluate others by the size of their deeds or because we feel that they are not 'pulling their weight'. Only God can see into the heart.

This teaching turns all our usual standards of 'good' and 'bad' upside down. But the writers of the *Formula of Concord* knew that they were merely teaching what the New Testament says: a healthy tree *must* bear good fruit; it cannot do anything else. A poor tree *must* bear bad fruit. A healthy tree *cannot* bear bad fruit. Nor can a poor tree bear good fruit (Matt 7:17,18; John 15:4,5,16; Jas 3:12). A person who makes a rule of following his or her selfish nature ('flesh') does the deeds of a selfish person. But those who belong to Christ in faith produce the 'fruit of the Spirit' (Gal 5:22–24). They cannot do anything else.

Faith has consequences

George Major, a Lutheran professor at Wittenberg, took careful note of texts like these and they made him uneasy. If faith automatically produces good deeds, people might begin to believe that God accepts them as they are even though they do as they like and revel in sin. Hadn't Luther himself stated that 'whoever does not perform such good works is a faithless man' (quoted p 553)? Following Luther, Major said faith must have consequences.

And here he was quite right. The *Formula of Concord* repeatedly states in Articles III and IV that it is a 'complacent . . . delusion' and 'impossible' to think that 'there could simultaneously be in a single heart both a right faith and a wicked intention to continue and abide in sin' (p 553; see also pp 474, 477, 545, 546, 550, 556). Faith involves our whole lives right down to the simplest questions of our private and professional behaviour.

Good works necessary for salvation?

But Major was not yet satisfied. People come to the astonished realisation that God has accepted them ('faith') and so they are new people (2 Cor 5:17). But if there are no real signs of a new life of good deeds in such people, Major asked, surely that must mean that they are not people with faith and are not saved. A person who has faith bears fruit. Surely that means that a person who does not bear fruit does not have faith either and so is cut off (Luke 3:8,9). Therefore, Major argued, good deeds are necessary for salvation.

His 'major' concern was that people should take their Christian lives much more seriously—and who can blame him for that? Indeed we could ask, Wouldn't we live more earnestly and strive more if we knew that our salvation ultimately depended on it?

The *Formula of Concord* admits that our Christian life is important: 'Good works are necessary' because God commands them (p 553). But it rejects the statement: 'Good works are necessary *for salvation*', because people might get the idea that

God accepts them because of their good deeds. It may be true that we banish God to the sidelines when we make our daily decisions and carry out our daily actions. But that doesn't mean we are lost, if we return to God day after day in repentance (p 543) and 'strive daily to lead a holy life' (*The Service—Alternative Form*). If Major had bothered to read Luke 13:6–9 he might have discovered that as long as we live, God in his mercy gives us another chance to be good trees (which do bear good fruit). And Major forgot that the greatest deed is to clutch at God and cry out: Lord, help me!

We don't have to go far in the churches and sects to find out what happens when Major's view is taken.

First danger: pharisaism

There have always been 'holiness' movements from the very beginning of the church's history. Like Major, they stress the individual life of the believer. They claim that a Christian who receives the Holy Spirit no longer sins. And so believers begin to judge their value not by what God says about them ('you are accepted!') but by the actions they see in themselves. If my good thoughts, words and deeds influence God's judgment of me, I will be tempted to look away from what Jesus Christ has done for me and examine myself and my spiritual life minutely.

That can be a very selfish thing. Some (not all!) Christians who give a personal testimony of their faith have spent so much effort looking at themselves that every sentence begins with 'I'. And then it's not long before you begin to evaluate your goodness by a pharisaical look at your apparently less virtuous neighbour (see Luke 18:11,12) and judge the faith of other Christians by the size and value of their deeds. The *Formula of Concord* therefore rejects Major's false views, because they 'confirm presumptuous trust in one's own righteousness and confidence in one's own good works' (p 555).

Second danger: building up credits

If good deeds were 'necessary for our salvation', it would also mean that we would have to spend all our efforts on improving our own life, not out of love to God, but so that *we* will be saved. And then we would be doing just what we are not meant to do. We would be acting in our *own* interests. In fact our 'good' deeds would no longer be good! If we worship God or visit a lonely person or make large contributions to the church or forgive someone after a quarrel for the sake of the credits we hope God will give us, these 'good' deeds become selfish and bad. We are using God and others to do ourselves a service.

The *Formula of Concord* reminds us that St Paul's words

> exclude our works and merit completely from the article of justification and salvation and ascribe everything solely to . . . the merit of Christ. (pp 554,555)

Third danger: doubt

Christians who believe that their good deeds count with God in the end can of course fall into the opposite trap. As they begin to examine their own lives they may discover that their best thoughts and actions are tainted with selfish motives. And then they may fall into great doubt about whether they belong to God at all, because they cannot see any great fruits of their faith.

For example, worry is a lack of trust in God and therefore a bad deed. But—taking Major's line—the more you worry the more you will be afraid of losing God. As a result you strive harder to suppress your worries. However, 1 Peter 5:7 doesn't tell you to suppress your worries but to 'leave all your worries with him, because he cares for you' (TEV)! God has accepted you in spite of your worrying. Just trust him!

The *Formula of Concord* rejects Major's views because they

> deprive tempted and troubled consciences of the consolation of the Gospel, give occasion for doubt . . . and are adopted . . . against the pure doctrine of salvation by faith alone. (p 555)

Fourth danger: the veneer of holiness

Society usually judges one's value by one's deeds and achievements. This seems to be so deeply ingrained in us that even as Christians we feel people will judge our faith by what they see. If good deeds are necessary for God's approval, as Major wrongly suggested, then we will want to make a good and holy impression on other Christians, otherwise they might come to think that God has not really accepted us.

Unfortunately, this danger is widespread, because people do tend to judge by the deeds they see—or by the sins. If a catastrophe strikes us, such as an illness or grave doubts, we feel we must put on a brave front. We may know that, in spite of everything we are going through, God is on our side, but we still feel we must put on a Sunday face along with our Sunday clothes.

Major's belief makes many people live in such pretence. You must smile, be brave, be friendly to all, show no 'unspiritual' emotions, such as a temper or irritability. You call your marital partner 'darling', but deep down there is resentment and anger. You feel that you must at least *show* that you are a good Christian and behave the way good Christians behave, even when your feelings are most unchristian. The result is a kind of Christian veneer.

Now, obviously, Christians are meant to struggle with their inner selves. But there is no struggle going on here; the sin of the heart is merely being covered up under a thin layer of piety.

This veneer of holiness, which is a face-saving device, is sometimes seen when Christians who normally speak just like everyone else adopt a 'holy' style of speech as soon as they are among church members. They use pious phrases to make a good impression. Pious phrases can be genuine. But they may be a sign of hollowness within. There is no need to play-act, since God accepts us as we are, without our deeds!

The *Formula of Concord* gives us great freedom here, which is like a breath of fresh air. It states bluntly:

> Such works of pretence God does not want . . . Truly good works are to be done willingly or from a spontaneous spirit by those whom the Son of God *has set free.* (p 554, emphasis mine)

What God thinks is decisive

In dealing with good deeds, the *Formula of Concord* makes other points which we must leave to the next chapter: Can we improve in our Christian life? Can we be sure we are accepted by God even when we commit the same sins again and again? Can God's gift of salvation be lost? What use is a Christian faith which makes no obvious difference to a Christian life?

But nobody can go wrong who understands the main thrust of the *Formula of Concord*. My Christian life is important. But when it comes to God accepting me, my life as a Christian does not count at all. I can never become more righteous and more holy than I already am when I receive Christ's righteousness in faith day by day. Justification by faith is God's *last* word (pp 548,554,557).

CHAPTER 7

Sinners and Saints

More and more countries today are sensitive to the problems of litter, waste and pollution—and to the need for preserving our natural environment. Yet when it comes to taking concrete steps to ban CFCs from aerosol sprays, some nations are not yet prepared to back up their policy with action. We rightly expect people to practise what they preach. A person who always spouts forth new ideas but makes no effort to implement them does not inspire confidence. And we all know how disappointed a child can be when promises made to it are not kept. Words must be backed up with actions, otherwise they are worthless.

Grace a soft pillow?

Anyone who looks for the main theme of the *Formula of Concord* will soon discover that it proclaims one single idea throughout: in spite of what you are God has accepted you.

That doctrine is not as popular as one might imagine. Some people claim that Lutherans make God's grace a soft pillow for lazy Christians. Why should they bother to practise what they preach if they are told again and again that they are fully accepted by God, although they are actually 'born failures'? So the critics accuse Lutherans of being interested merely in their own piety and their inner spiritual life. Is this true? Are Lutherans motivated by the undeserved grace of God to involve themselves in all the pressing problems of world peace, justice, ecology and starvation? Do we care about refugees, landmines, the disabled and AIDS sufferers?

Practising what we preach

A doctrine of justification which causes Christians to be complacent, idle and self-centred was the very last thing in the mind of St Paul or Luther—or *the Formula of Concord*. God's grace is not a 'cheap grace'. We do not receive God's gifts for our private enjoyment. They are meant to be used for the good of others. That is why St Paul is more interested in the practice of love than in the speaking of tongues (1 Cor 13:1). And the special point made in St Matthew's Gospel is to remind us that a Christian is to follow in Christ's footsteps.

Those who are accepted and forgiven by God are new people. They live by the Spirit in the power of Christ's love; and now it is self-understood that they will act as new people by that power (Gal 5:25). Or as the *Formula of Concord* puts it in Article III:

> After a person has been justified by faith, a true living faith becomes 'active through love' (Gal 5:6). Thus good works always follow justifying faith and are certainly to be found with it, since such faith is never alone but is always accompanied by love and hope. (p 474; see also p 546)

Personal piety or a life of love?

But we should not be too quick to dismiss the criticism sometimes levelled at Lutherans. In the past they have indeed often been guilty of silence on vital issues of the day. Many Lutherans are still uncertain whether contemporary issues like human rights or concern for the environment have anything to do with their faith. A careful look at any Lutheran hymn book shows how many hymns reflect an inward-looking, personal spirituality and how few deal with the Christian's life of love and responsibility. Occasionally, Lutherans still like to make a careful—and unlutheran—distinction between their 'spiritual' life and their 'normal' life.

It is good to remember here that Jesus came to deal with the whole person—body and soul. He fed the crowds not only in order to make a 'spiritual' point about being the bread of life (John 6:26–40) but also simply because they were hungry and he was desperately sorry for them (Mark 8:2,3). How deep is our concern for the two-thirds of our world who do not have enough to live on? How can we justify throwing away about twenty-five per cent of the food we buy (as we do), when not too far away people are clamouring for a handful of rice? Imagine what it would mean if we all reduced our weekly food bill by a mere twenty per cent and donated the proceeds to Lutheran World Service! Have we the right to consider what God does *for* us if we are not prepared to ponder what God wishes to do *through* us?

God calls us to act

Thus George Major's concern in 1552 was a genuine one. Surely, he asked, faith does not merely involve a private, cosy relationship between God and me; it involves my actions, my whole being. In a similar way Gerardus van der Leeuw once said: 'God calls us to be Christians, that is, to witness, to act . . . You do not become a Christian for what you can get out of it, but in order to act.'

Aren't we Christians often in danger of taking God's forgiveness for granted—and of living accordingly?

Good deeds not an optional extra

The Lutheran worship service can provide a corrective here. Often worship is seen only as the personal communion between God and Christians. But after hearing the promise of God's love and acceptance as preached in the sermon, Christians start looking beyond themselves and begin to look out into the world in which they will be called on to render 'divine service' in the week ahead. In our offerings we respond to God's grace by acting in a practical way for the benefit of others. We worship God by actions, not merely by words. (It is a mystery how well-to-do Christians in our society can still consider an offering of a dollar or two per week as an act of worship!)

The 'prayer of the church' also looks beyond personal needs. It is basically a prayer for others. As people confident of God's love and mercy, we begin our week of practical service by looking away from ourselves and praying for the needs of others—for all those we are preparing to serve. We bring before God the needs of the church and of missions, we pray for the political leaders of our nation. We consider those who are sick or in need and even pray for 'our arts and culture, our science and technology'.

Nor is the blessing simply an expression of the private relationship between God and us. Rather it is his promise of love and constant support as we leave the hour of calm and move out into a stormy, suffering world. There our divine service and worship is to continue under his blessing and with his power.

Article IV of the *Formula of Concord* on *Good Works* clearly states that good deeds are not an optional extra:

> We believe, teach, and confess . . . that all men, but especially those who are regenerated and renewed by the Holy Spirit, are *obligated* to do good works. (p 476, emphasis mine; see also p 553)

Failing the challenge

But what if we do not live in total service to God and to others? What if we fall into the same sins again and again? Can we be sure that we are still accepted by God?

All serious Christians have the experience that in spite of their best intentions and efforts they fail again and again to live up to the challenge of the gospel. We need only read the sermon on the mount or go through the ten commandments to realise that we always tend to consider ourselves and our own desires first. For example, we know perfectly well that worry is a lack of trust. When we worry we are doubting whether God really has our best interests at heart. And that sin in turn paralyses our life of Christian action. Yet we find ourselves worrying about the smallest things. Judged by the possibilities which the gospel opens up, there is not one single action we do which does not involve self-concern and lack of faith.

In the light of this we are tempted to ask: How can Christians be sure that God continues to accept them when their best efforts are only broken fragments?

Repeated forgiveness?

Worse still, there are those temptations which we cannot seem to master. Everyone has one or more particularly weak spots. Perhaps you know a particularly juicy piece of gossip about someone in the office and you are just dying to pass it on. Or you easily get impatient with other people. Or you have difficulty admitting you are wrong. Or your weak spot may be money or sex or alcohol. Whatever the case, you are tempted to deny by your actions what you really believe in and not to practise what you preach.

Surely God can't be expected to forgive us again and again when we repeatedly give way to these temptations. Surely if our actions are bad our faith must be bad too and we cannot be accepted by God. This was the line George Major took. If we are judged by our faith, he said, we are also judged by our actions, because faith and actions can't be separated.

In Article IV the *Formula of Concord* rejects this line of Major's and on the basis of texts like Romans 4:6–8 and Ephesians 2:8,9 makes the stupendous claim that although faith is never without actions (p 546), nevertheless God accepts us as we are:

> We believe, teach, and confess that good works should be excluded . . . from the article of our justification before God. (p 476)

And in Article III the *Formula of Concord* sharply criticises the idea

> that our justification before God is incomplete or imperfect without such love and renewal. (p 548)

The Christian: saint and sinner

The *Formula of Concord* can offer this great reassurance because this is the clear message of the New Testament. As a Christian I may be able to avoid certain sins, but I can't avoid sin. I remain a born failure. My whole life is a constant conflict between 'flesh' (my selfish nature) and the 'Spirit' (the new nature). One need only read Romans 7:14–25 or Galatians 5:17 to see how even St Paul knew of the failures in his Christian life: 'I don't do the good I want to do; instead, I do the evil that I do not want to do' (Rom 7:19 TEV).

On the basis of these texts Luther explained that believing Christians are saints and sinners at the same time. They are saints because they have been accepted by God; they are sinners because they constantly fail in their struggle against their selfish nature (*Luther's Works* 25,336). If God were to accept us on the basis of the life we live as Christians, no-one could 'stand before the tribunal of God' (p 545).

Improvement in the Christian life?

Since that's true, should we give up trying to practise what we preach? Can there be no improvement in the Christian life?

The New Testament is full of reminders to us that our lives of Christian love can and do grow. We may not always see that growth in ourselves. Luther says that Christians are like sick people under a doctor's care. The worst possible thing for them would be to imagine that they are healthy. In actual fact they are sick. But they are also 'healthy in hope and in the fact that they are beginning to be healthy' (*Luther's Works* 25,336). They may not feel they are getting well. If you lived in a dark house full of dust and cobwebs, it might look quite clean to you. But if someone were to come and light it up, the state of the house would give you a real shock. When Christ comes and lights up our lives we dare not be surprised at the mess his light reveals. Christians who see themselves in the brilliant light of Christ's holiness will be the last to notice any 'improvements' that have taken place in their lives. They will more likely be shocked at all the cobwebs. That's why I can't help being suspicious of Christians who are forever quoting examples of how clean their spiritual houses are.

Power for the Christian life

Yet we need not give up and resign ourselves to the fact that our houses aren't yet in order. For the Christian life is based on only one fact: God has *already* forgiven me because of Christ's death on the cross; his Easter victory has *already* destroyed the power of my sin. That means that as long as I trust God no improvement in my life—or apparent lack of it—can affect God's verdict on me which he gave on the cross: a sinner condemned with Christ—and therefore a saint accepted with Christ. Furthermore, Article III states:

> To those who by sheer grace, for the sake of the only mediator, Christ, through faith alone, without any work or merit, are justified before God (that is, accepted into grace) there is given the Holy Spirit, who renews and sanctifies them and creates within them love toward God and their fellowman. (p 543)

We can venture out into a stormy world and live our Christian lives, not on the strength of the goodness or piety we find in ourselves, but in the power of the Holy Spirit. That is why no Christian need resign in the face of repeated failure.

God's patience

In the sermon on the mount Jesus makes overwhelming demands on his followers and friends. They could easily give up in fright. But it is worth remembering that the sermon on the mount begins not with demands but with the beatitudes (Matt 5:3–11). There Jesus reminds us that first God loves and accepts the broken-hearted and the poor in spirit, who have no illusions about their own wretchedness and failure. For God can entrust his great works only to those who are utterly dependent on him. And his patience is greater than our failures: 'Whenever our hearts condemn us . . . God is greater than our hearts' (1 John 3:20).

The *Formula of Concord* takes the very same line:

> In the elect children of God this spontaneity [of good deeds] is not perfect, but they are still encumbered with much weakness . . . Nevertheless, for Christ's sake the Lord does not reckon this weakness against his elect, as it is written, 'There is therefore now no condemnation for those who are in Christ Jesus' (Rom 8:1). (p 477)

Daily repentance

In other words, the answer to constant failure in our Christian lives is not a desperate attempt at self-improvement but faith. God does not judge us on the success of our Christian life, as Major thought. What is required of us is simply to return to God again and again and 'keep on drowning the old nature . . . This happens when day after day we are sorry for the wrong things we have done and ask God to forgive us' (*Luther's Small Catechism,* p 27; see also 1 John 1:9).

One of the greatest passages of the Bible is Psalm 73:21–26: 'My flesh and my heart may fail' (v 26), but as long as I can cry to God in the midst of my crassest sins, 'Nevertheless, I am continually with you' (v 23), *all* is well. That 'nevertheless' is a defiant cry. It says that in spite of the mess I have made of my Christian life, I know and can declare, 'you hold my right hand' (v 23). And that means I can dare to persevere—even at the risk of failing again—and still know that I am accepted and my actions are good. Faith of this kind—and only faith—is the 'beginning, the middle and the end' of the whole Christian life (p 556).

The Christian life: a process

The Christian life is therefore never a time of calm and sweet rest and repose. 'We never *are* Christians in the sense that we have arrived and can now rest on our laurels. We are always *becoming* Christians' (George Forell). Christians do not live in an ivory tower. They go out into the world, knowing they will often fail. But they go out because they have to.

No young couple, after discovering each other, walk off into the sunset holding hands. Only fairytales suggest that they live happily ever after. If they are realistic they go into marriage knowing that they will have to make considerable adjustments to their relationship. But that doesn't prevent them from marrying. The Christian life is similar to that. Luther once wrote:

> So long as we live here on earth, believing in his Word, we are a work that God has begun, but not yet completed; but after death we shall be perfect . . . This life, therefore, is not godliness but the process of becoming godly, not health but getting well . . . not rest but exercise. We are not now what we shall be, but we are on the way. (*Luther's Works* 32,24; see also *Book of Concord*, pp 480,534)

St Paul says we are to be like athletes who must keep in strict training if we don't wish to lose the prize (1 Cor 9:24–27; see also *Book of Concord*, p 554).

But we are not pessimists. We know that eventually we will win in this struggle because of the power of Christ given to us in his word and the sacraments. I may not see growth in my life as a Christian—but it will certainly be there. For wherever there is this kind of faith, there *are* good deeds!

Dead faith?

Can God's gift of salvation be lost? The *Formula of Concord* stresses that there is such a thing as a 'dead faith' (p 553), so that a person sins deliberately. People caught in a snowstorm are often stricken with an overwhelming desire to sleep. They have to struggle to keep awake. Whoever succumbs to sleep won't wake up again. St Paul's cry in Ephesians 5:14 was aimed at sleeping Christians—those who deliberately give way to temptation without a struggle, as well as those who take God's forgiveness in Christ so much for granted that they echo Voltaire's sentiments, 'God will forgive me. It's his job.' No, it's not his job; it's his grace. We dare not use God as something we put away for a rainy day.

Another chance

But a sleeper can still be woken up!

When we are watching, should sleep overtake us,
Jesus, we ask you, sustain and awake us.

('Help us to conquer, Thou Prince ever-living')

The Christian who can do no more than stammer these words remains one of God's saints—and a power for good in a broken world.

CHAPTER 8

For Christ's Sake, Yes!

It is a common experience in times of unemployment: you answer the front door and are confronted by an unshaven man in shabby clothes. He has the offer of a job in the country, he tells you, and needs twenty dollars to get there. A telephone call soon confirms his story. What should you do?

You might decide to act in one of the following ways. You might say to yourself, 'Nobody gets anything for nothing. This man can earn the money he needs.' You remember the weeds in the back garden. So you say to him, 'If you clean up my garden, then I'll pay you for it'. After three hours the man leaves with his twenty dollars, and you feel quite satisfied with your act of 'Christian' love. But what have you actually done? You have put conditions on your help: 'If . . . then . . .' *If* people want my help, *then* they have to earn it.'

Alternatively, in this situation you might say to yourself, 'Because this man is in need, therefore I'll help. But it must put a dent in one's self-respect to have to go around begging. I'll let him do a bit of gardening and pay him twenty dollars at the end. Then he won't be dependent on my "generosity".' What have you done here? There are no conditions for your help: 'Because . . . therefore . . .' *Because* you care, *therefore* you help. You would give the man the money anyway. It really is a gift. The gardening is merely your way of protecting his self-respect.

Conditions or gift?

Two identical actions—a man has come asking for money, and you have given it to him after he has done some gardening—but what a world of difference in the attitudes and motives! In the first case help depends on conditions (*if . . . then . . .*). This is the approach of *law.* If you reach a certain level of performance or achievement, then you are acceptable—and only then.

In the second case there are no conditions. Help has been given freely (*because . . . therefore . . .*). The New Testament calls this kind of approach *gospel.* Because I love you, therefore I accept you—whether your performance level is satisfactory or not.

The law approach tries to motivate people to act in a certain way by holding up rewards or punishments. To a child: *If* you're a good boy, *then* I'll take you to the zoo. To a husband or wife: *If* you are more considerate to me, *then* I'll be nice to you.

The gospel approach reminds us that we are accepted *first*, and therefore there are no conditions to be met. We act on the basis of being accepted first. To a child: *Because* I love you, *therefore* I'll take you to the zoo. To a husband or wife: *Because* God has entrusted you into my care, *therefore* I'll be nice to you—and make every effort to find a solution to our problem that suits us both.

Distinguishing law and gospel

The example of the unemployed man shows, however, that it is not at all easy to distinguish between a law approach and a gospel approach. What seems to count are the attitudes and motives behind an action. In certain situations it may not seem to matter very much. Whether I keep to the speed limit because I am afraid of punishment ('law') or because I am concerned for the welfare of other road users ('gospel') is unimportant as far as the police are concerned. The police are usually not interested in my motives.

In the area of God's relationship to us, however, the distinction between law and gospel is vital. The repeated questions of concerned Christians show that there is a great deal of uncertainty about this distinction. As someone once said to me, 'I often wonder what God really thinks of us. How do I know whether he is really pleased with us?' Does God make conditions which I have to fulfil before he can be pleased with me?

These are some of the difficult questions which the *Formula of Concord* in Article V on *Law and Gospel* helps us to answer. For unless we can distinguish law and gospel in God's word we will never know where we stand with God. Does God use the law approach with us (*if . . . then . . .*)? Or does he approach us with the gospel and simply tell us that we are accepted? Or does he mix the two and tell us that we're accepted—*if* we are 'sincere' about him and *if* we try to do our best?

Keeping the law

When we think of God's law we naturally think of the ten

commandments (Exod 20:2–17). Ancient Israel saw these laws as a gift of God. Through them he protects the world and keeps it functioning smoothly in spite of our sin. This law is therefore good.

Of course, if you can keep those laws you have no problems—or so it would seem. Nobody has to murder, steal, be unfaithful in marriage or talk about people behind their backs. Social custom may countenance mild deception in the matter of income tax returns ('everyone does it'), but you *can* be honest in this area if you wish.

Law produces arrogance

The difficulties arise, as St Paul discovered, when we 'religious' people believe we have fulfilled the conditions God lays down. For then we imagine that God accepts us because we have earned his reward. Everyone knows the smug feeling one can have when one has resisted the temptation to make a cutting remark, or has restored a lost purse or wallet to its owner. God's law is good—but I tend to misuse it as an excuse for blowing my own trumpet. And that means that I am keeping from God the very thing he wants most of all: the trust of my heart! Jesus' radical explanation of the commandments in Matthew 5:21–28 shows that God does not ask, 'What did you do?' but, 'Where was your heart when you did it?' (pp 559,560). If I withhold from God the trust of my heart, I have broken the most important commandment of all: the first commandment (see *Luther's Large Catechism*, pp 103–5!).

St Paul therefore reserves the brunt of his criticism (Rom 2:1 – 3:20) not for the atheists but for 'religious' people—be they of Jewish, Roman Catholic, charismatic or even Lutheran vintage. For it is the *religious* people who are most likely to imagine that God is just as pleased with them as they are with themselves. They take their religious life so seriously that they are no longer 'helpless before God'. As Luther rather coarsely put it, they 'contemplate their navels'. Jesus' parable of the Pharisee and the tax collector (Luke 18:10–14) should teach us that even the praise of God can be an exercise in self-righteousness.

Therefore religious people are no better than rank atheists. Both withhold from God the honour due to him: '*All* have sinned' (Rom 3:23).

Law produces despair

That is why the law is necessary: to reveal sin (Rom 3:19,20). It shows me that at the very moment when I think I am keeping God's law I am actually relying on myself. And then I am godless. So God's law brings me to the point of utter helplessness. There is nothing in myself to fall back on—no good intentions are acceptable to God, no acts of kindness, no religious feelings, no acceptance of church doctrines. For as soon as I look at what is in *me*, my eyes are turned away from God. And that means I am breaking the first commandment, which expects 'a person's whole heart and full confidence in God alone and in no one else' (*Luther's Large Catechism*, p 21). No wonder the law produces despair if I take it seriously.

The *Formula of Concord* summarises the whole problem succinctly:

> As long as men hear only the law and hear nothing about Christ . . . they become either conceited hypocrites, like the Pharisees, or they despair, as Judas did. (pp 478,479; see also p 559)

The curse of the law

That is the terrible either/or we all face daily—either arrogance or despair. And both are a denial of God! To live under the law is therefore to live under God's curse (Gal 3:10). As Luther wrote in his famous Galatians commentary, 'The law always accuses and damns' (*Luther's Works* 27,16; see *Book of Concord*, p 150). It teaches a person 'to know his sin' (p 560); it points out the problems in our relationship to God, but it does not remove them. It makes an excellent diagnosis but can provide no cure. St Paul makes no bones about where we stand with God in the light of his law: 'No one is put right with God by means of the Law' (Gal 3:11 TEV).

If we know that preaching or laying down the law only produces arrogance or despair and does not correct sin but merely exposes it, we will have good reason as Christian parents or teachers to rethink our use of law towards children. You cannot make people better by making demands on them. Or if you lay down the law with your husband or wife you must be clear about what you're really doing. You may be exposing their faults, but you're only producing defiance or resignation.

No conditions to the gospel

One thing is clear: When God accepts me and is pleased with me—and that is the basic message of the whole Bible—it is obviously *without any conditions at all.* He obviously accepts me as I am—not *if* I at least try to do my best, not *if* I am sincere about him, not *if* I am in despair through his law, not *if* I am ready for him, not even *if* I accept the fact that I need God's help. People who have heard or felt the full force of God's law are crushed; they are in no position to fulfil any conditions. A person lying in hospital with both legs in plaster is helpless.

But now we are in the area of the gospel and here no conditions apply. The only thing that applies here is God's statement: 'Because I love you and have accepted you in Christ, therefore you are accepted. All is well.' The *Formula of Concord* echoes this statement clearly:

> The content of the Gospel is this, that the Son of God, Christ our Lord, himself assumed and bore the curse of the law and expiated and paid for all our sins, that *through him alone* we re-enter the good graces of God, obtain forgiveness of sins through faith, are freed from death and all the punishments of sin, and are saved eternally. (p 561, emphasis mine; see also p 478)

Christ fulfils law's conditions

The conditions and threats of God's law no longer apply to us, because Christ has suffered the law's punishments for all people and so has fulfilled all God's conditions. On the cross the punishment of God's law strikes him, not us. We are out of the storm of law and punishment, sailing on the calm waters of the gift, promise, gospel.

Christ the living gospel

What is the gospel like? Jesus Christ is the living example of the gospel approach. You expect him to deal with evil, godless people the way a sectarian preacher does: throw the book at them; drive out their sins. Certainly there are threats—here Christ applies God's law. But they are aimed at the self-satisfied and self-righteous who are quite certain of their superior status in God's eyes (John 9:39–41).

Jesus seems to prefer spending his time with fairly hopeless types, by any standards: embezzlers, adulterers, even a political revolutionary. According to God's law the evil his friends have done would have to be paid for. But instead he sits down with them without reproach, without conditions. He simply treats them as friends. And this is God! When he gets around to speaking of their sins there is sadness in his voice, but not the thunder of the prophet, and they feel no need to squirm (John 4:17,18).

He simply tells them their sins are forgiven (Mark 2:5; Luke 7:47,48). 'Do not be afraid, little flock, for it is your Father's *good pleasure* to give you the kingdom' (Luke 12:32). And that is said to the very disciples who are people 'of little faith' (Luke 12:28)! No conditions! A gift!

Comfort of the gospel

His parables have the same message. God's law sets up a barrier between good and bad. Jesus removes the barrier and invites to his Father's celebration 'both good and bad' (Matt 22:10).

The bad boy decides to go home, but even before he can stammer his few words of repentance—*he* thinks that is a condition for his father to accept him!—his dignified father does something no Oriental would ever do: he *runs out* to meet him, throws his arms around him and hugs him for dear life—*before* his son can even recite the little piece he has rehearsed so carefully. And when he finally does get around to saying it, his father hardly seems to listen. He is much too busy and excited planning a big homecoming party (Luke 15:20–24).

The workers in the vineyard still want to earn their reward. How naive! They have to learn that because God accepts them as they are they have received incomparably more generous wages than they could ever get on any other labour market, where you get what you deserve (Matt 20:1–15).

Jesus not only proclaims the gospel; he is the gospel. He not only promises forgiveness; he is forgiveness. And all those in union with him live in and by the gospel. Therefore our words and actions are taken into the gospel, for

> everything which comforts and which offers the mercy and grace of God to transgressors of the law . . . is . . . the Gospel, a good and joyful message that God wills not to punish sins but to forgive them for Christ's sake. (pp 561,562)

The comfort lies in the fact that no ifs can ever apply again to Christians—unless they are arrogant enough to try to impress God. And then the law will blast them back in Christ's direction again!

God's yes

Does God make conditions I have to fulfil in order to please him? Not for those who, overwhelmed by the message of the gospel (faith), can put their 'confidence solely on the Lord Jesus Christ' (p 562). What does God really think of us? Is he pleased with us? For Christ's sake, yes!

It was Luther who stated that God's law has one main purpose: it is God's 'strange' way of bringing us again and again to the point where he can help us, accept us. His 'real' work is gospel (pp 479,560).

Are you worried about your motives for acting? You are told that in spite of your failures and sins Christ's cross and resurrection cast their light—and forgiveness—on everything you do! 'Jesus Christ . . . is not one who is "Yes" and "No". On the contrary, he is God's "Yes" ' (2 Cor 1:19 TEV).

In spite of my constant failures I can dare to be confident. I need not lose courage. I know where I stand with God. I know through God's law that I am condemned. But I know through the gospel that I am accepted. And because God came to this world in Jesus Christ, it is the gospel that counts.

Therefore it is vital that we learn to distinguish between law and gospel in God's word. If we never learnt the difference,

> this would darken the merit of Christ and rob disturbed consciences of the comfort which they would otherwise have in the holy Gospel when it is preached purely and without admixture, for by it Christians can support themselves in their greatest temptations against the terrors of the law. (p 558; see also pp 479,563)

God's yes is stronger than his no.

CHAPTER 9

Jesus Only

At some time every person has to learn not to take for granted what he or she treasures and values. The important things in life, even when they are ours, can easily be lost through neglect. Married couples soon discover that their love needs constant renewal if it is not to become dull and lifeless. You can say 'I love you' a thousand times and yet never know what love really is.

Similarly the most flourishing democracy can turn into a system of oppression and discrimination, unless politicians and voters are constantly testing their democratic values. One can use phrases like 'our democratic way of life' and yet curtail the very freedoms and rights one is meant to uphold.

Need to rediscover the gospel

The *Formula of Concord* suggests in Article V on *Law and Gospel* that much the same is true in the church. Lutherans are proud of the Reformation rediscovery of the pure gospel—that God accepts us in Jesus Christ through faith; we do not win his approval. But it is possible to say the right words and celebrate Luther's memory with fanfares—and yet to put conditions on the gospel. There is a danger that we turn gospel into law.

The *Formula of Concord* apparently regarded this danger as very real. Why else would it stress that we must observe the distinction between law and gospel with 'particular diligence lest we . . . change the Gospel into law' (p 558; see also p 478)? Apparently it is very easy to drift into speaking the gospel as though there were conditions! Therefore each age and each Christian must rediscover what the gospel is.

The Hammer of God

That is the theme of a powerful and moving novel, *The Hammer of God*, by Bo Giertz. Bishop Giertz describes a young pastor's discovery of the gospel—without conditions.

For years he has been preaching the gospel as though it were law. He believes that the way to a life acceptable to God is by self-denial and obedience to Christ. He says, in effect, *if* we struggle against our sin, *then* God will accept us. There are conditions. And so his 'gospel' is no gospel at all. As a result, Pastor Fridfeldt's converts are either discouraged or self-righteous. The law always does that.

One Sunday morning, Fridfeldt is called to the bedside of a dying man named Frans who is known for his piety. On the edge of unconsciousness Frans's mind wanders and, to the pastor's horror, he begins to speak of an evil past, jealousy, revenge, self-righteous pride—all interspersed with vulgar language. 'Beneath the thin shell of his conscious faith this evil still dwelt within the heart . . . The lid had fallen off, and everything lay bare' (*The Hammer of God*, pp 195,196).

The young pastor is horrified because he knows he himself is no better. How much of people's old sinful nature could be left in them! 'If such a man could be saved, on what grounds would it be? His faith? But that, as they had seen, was gone at the same moment that his consciousness clouded; and behind it all the sin lay in ferment to the very end' (p 199). God's law demands that we get better and better. But what happens when we discover that all our old evil lurks in the depths? If God accepts me because of my sincerity, what do I do when I discover that this sincerity is only a pious veneer? Those are the terrible questions Fridfeldt asks himself.

The gospel in a nutshell

He finds his answer that day and discovers the gospel. It is the same answer old Frans had uttered in the last moments of consciousness. His daughter had said to him, 'You are still thinking about Jesus, are you not, Father?' And he had replied, 'I am not able to, Lena. I can't think any longer. But I know Jesus is thinking of me' (pp 193,194).

That is the gospel in a nutshell, unmixed with law. Frans is a Christian who dies in grace, in spite of the dirt in his heart! Fridfeldt discovers the same message in Matthew 17:8: 'And when they looked up, they saw no one but *Jesus only'*. Not obedience, not repentance, not devotion, not piety is the path to God's heart, but—Jesus *only*! He has done it all.

The 'legal gospel'

How can we then dare to make any statement as Christians which does not end in the two words: Jesus only? How can we dare to state the gospel as though it were law? Throughout the world the ifs of Christians continue to fly thick and fast, the ifs of the 'legal gospel'—that is no gospel at all:

- If you really have faith, God will care for you.
- If you are sincere, God will be on your side.
- If you give up this or that you can be regarded as a true Christian.
- If you really pray fervently, God will give you what you ask.
- If you trusted more in God your troubles/worries/sickness would be over.

Those ifs and others like them—whether they come from holiness movements in the church, from the theology of social concern or from the preacher who pounds the pulpit most on Reformation Day—are the greatest enemy of the gospel of God's grace in Christ, for what God does is made to depend on what we do.

Nobody in the church will object to faith, self-sacrifice, prayer, trust, social concern or true doctrine. But God does not accept us because of these. They are the results of the gospel, not its conditions.

Luther felt very strongly about this. In a sermon of 1532 he attacks those who

> talk a lot about faith but they mix things together . . . by saying if you live in such and such a way God will be gracious to you, and they turn the mercy seat into a judgment seat and the judgment seat into a mercy seat. (*Luther's Works*, 51,283)

Luther is not backward in saying what he thinks of these ifs. He calls them 'idle wish-wash' (*Luther's Works*, 51,286)!

Faith a condition?

But once again the question arises: Surely we cannot be accepted by God without faith? Is it not important how we feel and how sincere we are? Above all, doesn't the *Formula of Concord* itself make conditions when it says:

> *If* they [sinners] believe the Gospel God forgives them all their sins through Christ, accepts them for his sake as God's children, and out of pure grace . . . justifies and saves them. (*Book of Concord*, p 563, emphasis mine)

Is it possible that the writers of the *Formula of Concord* themselves were unable to distinguish between law and gospel?

I believe they would have been shocked if someone had

accused them of putting conditions on God's grace. The problem lies really with us, not with them. For them faith meant simply confidence in Christ, not in themselves. Faith was not a quality or a feeling of pious devotion which could earn anything. Faith was suddenly to know: What God has done *means me*. Faith was a gift of God, not some kind of religious effort on our part.

Faith a good deed?

The trouble is that many Christians no longer see faith like that. They regard faith as sincerity or religious feelings or commitment to a cause or belief in certain teachings. Faith for modern people (unlike the Reformation) is a desirable deed you do so that God will let you off all the other things he really expects of you. It is seen as a kind of payment for God's favours.

This obviously means that today we cannot simply repeat the formulas of the *Formula of Concord* to understand what is meant by the gospel. I can say 'justification by faith alone', but often what I really mean is justification by my sincerity, justification by my feelings, justification because I have given my heart to Jesus (see *The Hammer of God*, p 146), or even justification by my acceptance of the doctrine of justification by faith. I only need Jesus in order to get his approval of what *I* have done for him. The *Formula of Concord* warns us that all this serves only to 'darken the merits and benefits of Christ' and 'once more make the Gospel a teaching of law' (*Book of Concord*, p 563).

Is my faith acceptable to God?

Above all, the *Formula of Concord* brings up its old argument against this 'legal gospel' which can only 'rob Christians of the true comfort which they have in the Gospel against the terrors of the law' (p 563). There is really nothing to prevent me devoting my life to the alleviation of misery and a more equal distribution of the world's wealth. But how do I set about learning to *believe*? That can be the most impossible deed of God's law to fulfil, for I can never know whether I believe enough for God. And then the terrible question arises: Am I accepted by God? Is my faith up to scratch? Can I ever be sure? This was precisely Luther's agonising problem when he was a monk.

And then it is utterly useless to tell people that God loves them for Christ's sake, if you turn around and say with the next breath that they have to feel it or be sincere or 'believe'. For that is the one thing they cannot do. They simply need to be told again and again: God has accepted you in Christ. The rest can be left up to the Holy Spirit, who creates, not sincerity or pious feelings or self-satisfaction, but *faith*.

At the end of all his struggles Luther did not discover in himself an ability to believe. He discovered nothing—in himself. He discovered—no, the Holy Spirit gave him the discovery—'Jesus only'. His eyes were opened and he suddenly knew: That is faith! That is the gospel!

Faith as poverty of spirit

Luther meant something like this when he said that God is closer to us than our own skin. He is certainly closer to us than our feelings, sincerity, conditions. And this is the very same thing the *Formula of Concord* wants us to understand when it says that

> every penitent sinner . . . must put his confidence solely on the Lord Jesus Christ . . . who was 'made our righteousness' (1 Cor 1:30). (p 562)

Jesus only! Nothing in me! Bo Giertz summarises what faith is and captures the secret of the gospel:

> Faith does not dwell in our brain and in our thoughts. Faith is not a work we accomplish; it is not a gift we give to God. Being made righteous by faith does not imply that faith is some kind of payment that will serve as well as our . . . good works . . . Faith is . . . a poverty of spirit . . . a poor, empty heart opening toward God. (*The Hammer of God*, p 217)

Righteousness is based on Christ, not on the 'believer'. God does not accept me as a reward for believing in him. I believe in him and trust him because he has accepted me. Luther found his trust and his feelings uncertain. But in times of struggle and doubt he took out a piece of chalk and wrote on his desk in Latin: *baptizatus sum*, I am baptised! God has accepted me! And that is true whether I feel it or not. God has accepted me. That is all that counts.

Infant baptism is pure gospel

How else could we baptise infants? We baptise them not because of their sincerity or feelings or because they have 'let Jesus into their lives'. We baptise them because God accepts them in baptism. A baby is united with Christ. A sinner is declared a saint. Those who deny the validity of infant baptism and demand a prior decision of faith as a condition for baptism are making law out of the gospel.

But even many a Lutheran pastor finds it hard to baptise the infant of parents who merely want their child 'done' and have no contact with the church. Often here the legalist in the pastor wants to take over. A former bishop of the Lutheran Church of Norway, faced with similar questions, asked: Can an infant be given a savings account with, say, five thousand dollars in it? Does its value depend on whether the child is able to assess its value? The answer is obvious. Of course an infant can receive a valuable present, long before it can understand or use it. So God can give the great gift of forgiveness, acceptance and life to a little child before it can evaluate the size of the gift.

It is in infant baptism that the gospel is proclaimed loudest in the church; for here it is quite clear that in God's sight we are beings who *receive*. That is what Jesus meant when he said, 'Whoever does not receive the kingdom of God as a little child will never enter it' (Mark 10:15). A child shows what real faith means: to be in God's presence with empty hands, to be dependent on God. Someone once said: what God does in baptism is to put a big plus sign in front of the bracket of our lives. We are placed on a level with every other Christian. And God does this *before* it is evident to anybody who we will be and what we will be like. Everywhere else in the world we are assessed on our performance and achievements. God does it the other way around. For Jesus' sake and because of *his* performance, God assesses us on the basis of his love, *before* we even have a chance to start achieving. What could be more gospel-like than that? Jesus only!

Need for God's law

Of course there is still an important place in the church for the preaching of God's law. But its purpose is not to lay down conditions for God's approval. What God's law does is to bring sinful people to the point where they really learn to know their sin (*Book of Concord*, p 560) and their need for God's loving help.

Strictly speaking, God's law is not there to improve people or make the world a better place to live in. Its main task is to make people realise that they are helpless when they try to reach God on their own—because they can never fulfil the conditions which God's law demands. As the *Formula of Concord* puts it, 'the Holy

Spirit through the office of the law rebukes the unbelief involved in man's failure to believe in Christ' (p 561). As long as we are 'indifferent and secure' (p 559), the law accuses us. But those who are helpless and oppressed and know their failures before God do not need his law preached at them. They need large doses of the gospel.

Confusing law and gospel

There are countless ways in which law and gospel can be confused. When Jesus is regarded merely as an example I am to follow, the gospel is mixed with law. There are conditions to be met. When Christians try to frighten people into believing, the gospel becomes law. The fact is that Jesus came preaching: 'Repent, for the kingdom of heaven has come near' (Matt 4:17). He did not say: 'Repent, for the gates of hell are upon you'. It is God's kindness that is meant to lead to repentance (Rom 2:4), not his wrath. The *Formula of Concord* repeats that 'the preaching of the law is not sufficient for genuine and salutary repentance; the Gospel must also be added to it' (p 561).

When preachers make a principle of reducing expectant or timid Christians on Sunday mornings to heaps of misery before reminding them in a reproving tone that Jesus died for their sins, they are mixing law and gospel. They need not be surprised if their hearers depart more depressed than when they came. Even the preaching of the cross of Christ can be, as the *Formula of Concord* reminds us, 'an earnest and terrifying preaching . . . of God's wrath which really directs people into the law' and is not therefore 'the preaching of the Gospel but the preaching of Moses and the law' (p 479). The pastor who preaches the gospel as though it contained some indirect, hidden threat fails to preach it altogether. For to say in effect, 'God will be merciful to you, if only you have fully recognised how deeply you need God', or, worse still, 'if only you show through your actions how sincere your faith is', is to preach not the gospel but the law. For then I would be expected to do something for God first before God can help me.

God's real work

God chose in Jesus Christ to open himself up to us and to accept us on the basis of forgiveness and love (gospel), rather than on the basis of commands and demands (law), which we would have had to fulfil. And so the *ultimate* task of any Christian is to proclaim the gospel, to speak of God's love and forgiveness and to spread comfort and hope. Certainly the law will need to be applied—to those who are clearly complacent and self-righteous. But as the *Formula of Concord* states (quoting Luther), God's judgment through his law is his 'alien work' (pp 479,560). Judgment and threats are not God's normal way of dealing with us. They are God's way of bringing us to the point where he can get at us. For the incredible comfort of the gospel will only get through to us when the demands of the law have convinced us that we cannot live up to them. There is no hope for us if God starts assessing us on our performance. God can help us only when we have given up trying to help ourselves.

God's normal way of dealing with us—Christ's 'proper office' (p 479)—is love, 'to preach grace, to comfort, to make alive' (p 479). People who are convinced that God is punishing them for something they have done should take comfort from this! They must remind themselves again and again that God only engages in his 'alien work' of punishment and anger through his law to prepare us for his *real* work of love, grace and comfort through the gospel. God's anger through his law is merely the other side of his love in the gospel. That's why we dare not preach God's law as though it were gospel, or preach the gospel as though it were law!

Keeping law and gospel apart

Law and gospel are both necessary. But we must be clear on the difference. God's law demands. The gospel gives and bids us to 'hold out our hands and to receive what is being offered' (*Luther's Works* 26,208). God's law makes us consider our own needs and makes us selfish. The gospel takes us away from ourselves and opens us for God and for all the need of our suffering world. God's law makes me do good for my own advantage—another pearl for my heavenly crown. The gospel frees me to look away from myself and notice the need of others. The law makes the church inward-looking, prim and smug, concerned only for its purity and the preservation of its structures and traditions. The gospel makes the church a dynamic instrument of God's goodwill towards the world. The law gives rise to self-righteous Pharisees separate from the world. The gospel creates humble servants in the world. The law kills initiative and imagination. The gospel makes creative and courageous. For the gospel says that the whole meaning of life lies not in our hands but in the hands of—Jesus only!

CHAPTER 10

Blueprint for Action

Anyone who has caught a glimpse of the freedom and joy of the gospel will be puzzled at the waning interest in the Christian message among the majority of people today.

One of the reasons for this indifference is that Christians have not succeeded in making clear to ordinary men and women what the church really stands for. We have given the general public rules of behaviour and solid middle-class values. We have been excellent advertisements of the law. But we have failed to live the gospel.

The church as guardian of morals

As a result, the image many people have of the church and its message is negative. The church is often seen as a guardian of morals, making sure that people keep on the straight and narrow. From the outside, Christian faith can appear as a list of oppressive dos and don'ts. A church with this kind of image will attract neither those who consider that they already live a decent life nor those who feel that they cannot measure up to the moral standards of middle-class church members. It sometimes certainly seems as though Christians are more interested in making people behave themselves than they are in caring for the underprivileged.

Of course there are times when the church *must* speak out, for example when new laws place human life under threat, or when government policies encourage economic growth at the cost of economic justice for all. God has laid down basic laws 'to maintain external discipline and decency against dissolute and disobedient people', as the *Formula of Concord* states in Article VI on *the Third Function of the Law* (p 563). Through these laws God preserves the world from total chaos in areas such as marriage, the family, political life and the economy. Society has the responsibility of preserving these basic structures under God's law. The church cannot remain silent when these basic structures are under threat or are even set aside completely.

Fail-safe rules?

However, many people criticise the church because they can

see only the finger raised in warning, while the New Testament preaches the gospel of the arms stretched out in love. Is this criticism justified? Is it possible that we Christians prefer to preach the law rather than live under the gospel?

If the criticism is justified at all, it is certainly not because the *gospel* is like that, but because we are. The gospel begins with God's statement, 'I have called you by name, you are mine' (Isa 43:1). But instead of taking that statement at face value and simply living in faith, we imagine that there are all kinds of additional duties and laws that are required of us to be 'good' Christians. And we certainly like others to be like us.

Secretly we like laws. Don't we secretly think that a person who manages to keep five of the ten commandments is better in God's eyes that the person who keeps none? Besides, deep down we prefer Moses to Christ. Laws give us security; we know where we stand. People who have spent half a lifetime in jail, living by prison regulations, are often helpless when they are released. Their new freedom frightens them. Many Christians are like that. They are afraid of the new freedom the gospel gives them to make their day-to-day decisions in faith and love to God. They become uneasy if they do not know exactly what is expected of them in every situation. They are not satisfied with general Christian guidelines. They expect the Bible or their pastor to provide them with a fail-safe rule for every conceivable situation. It is much safer that way. For some legalistic Christians laws are a good substitute for complete trust in the power of the Holy Spirit!

Christian freedom

The *Formula of Concord* serves the gospel because it repeatedly stresses that we can dare to be absolutely certain of God's love and acceptance in Christ, whether we deserve it or not and irrespective of how many of the commandments we manage to keep or not. Our achievements—and our failures—no longer count with God.

That message the church should be proclaiming loudly and clearly in public. In Jesus Christ we are free—free to forget ourselves, our achievements, failures, worries, fears. He has taken care of all that. If 'nothing can separate us from his love' (Rom 8:38 TEV), we are free from having to worry about whether we have done enough to please God. God is on our side, supporting us in every aspect of life. We can put everything into his loving hands and live as free people, because in Christ's death and resurrection God has proved that he will never let us down.

Instead of living by our old nature under all of God's crushing rules, we live in the freedom of the Spirit. 'Where the Spirit of the Lord is, there is freedom' (2 Cor 3:17). 'Freedom is what we have—Christ has set us free! Stand, then, as free people, and do not allow yourselves to become slaves again' (Gal 5:1 TEV). People who have to live by their achievements and successes—and so are always afraid of the future—are no better than slaves. St Paul never wearies of reminding his readers that in baptism they have received the Spirit. God has come to them in person, and his is not a spirit of slavery bringing fear back into their lives, but a Spirit who makes them free children of God (Rom 8:15).

A blow for freedom

In Article VI the *Formula of Concord* follows the New Testament in striking a blow for freedom:

> When a person is born anew by the Spirit of God and is liberated from the law . . . he does everything from a free and merry spirit. (p 566)

Christians do good deeds not by blindly following a new set of regulations. They

> have been freed and liberated from the curse of the law. (p 564)

Rather,

> in so far as they are reborn,

they do good deeds

> as spontaneously as if they knew of no command, threat, or reward. (p 481)

The Christian faith is not a new list of dos and don'ts. It is the freedom of knowing that we are doing God's will whenever we act in trust.

This is what the *Formula of Concord* means when it states:

> Christians are not under the law but under grace because their persons have been freed from the curse and condemnation of the law through faith in Christ. Though their good works are still imperfect and impure, they are acceptable to God through Christ because according to their inmost self they do what is pleasing to God not by coercion of the law but willingly and spontaneously from the heart by the renewal of the Holy Spirit. (pp 567,568)

Do Christians need God's law?

Does the Christian then need God's law at all? If we are Christians who 'live by the Spirit' (Gal 5:25), won't we automatically do what God wants? This was the difficult question raised by some Lutheran pastors and professors after 1527. John Agricola said there was no place for the law in the church at all, since the gospel has replaced it. Anton Otto—or probably one of his over-zealous followers—claimed that the Christian is above God's law and no longer needs to obey it. Andreas Musculus even suggested that Luther was not 'Lutheran' enough, while Michael Neander wondered whether a Christian needs a guide on how to live the Christian life.

These were serious questions, and in one way or another they are still being raised today. If Christ is the 'end of the law' (Rom 10:4) and Christians are free (John 8:36; Gal 5:1), does God's law really apply to them? Are there dos and don'ts after all? And how are we to explain the long lists of commands and admonitions of Jesus and St Paul?

The clouded vision

Luther already suggested the answer to these questions in 1539 when he wrote about Agricola and his followers: 'It seems to me that these spirits think that all who are listening to the message are pure Christians, without sin' (*Luther's Works* 47,111). It is true that our failures and our selfishness no longer count in God's eyes; we are accepted. God's law can never condemn us as long as we know that. Once and for all: You do not have to fulfil rules and conditions to be regarded by God as a good Christian. Your 'sins are covered up through the perfect obedience of Christ' (*Book of Concord*, p 565). Therefore the law can make no further demands on you. You are free.

The trouble is that we are not only accepted saints; we are also self-centred sinners and we do not always automatically love God and others. And so, when it comes to recognising what God's will is in any situation, our vision is clouded:

> If believers . . . were perfectly renewed in this life through the indwelling Spirit . . . they would do what they are obligated to do . . . spontaneously and unhindered . . . But in this life Christians are not renewed perfectly and completely. (pp 564,565)

Therefore they need God's commands 'to light their way' (p 480).

Obeying God's commands

God's commands are an expression of his will for us. The commands of his law—such as the ten commandments or the admonitions of St Paul—show us imperfect Christians the appropriate way to live and act when we live under the gospel. We do not try to obey these divine commands in order to win another pearl for our heavenly crown. Since Christ died for us there is no more room for pearls on our heavenly crown, as Helmut Thielicke once put it. No, we seek to obey the commands of God's law simply because we want to live *his* life and do what *he* wants.

A standard for free decision

This does not mean that our Christian freedom is curtailed. Christians do have the freedom to decide what God wants them to do 'in so far as they are reborn' (p 481) and to make their decisions totally in faith to God. But because 'the conflict between flesh and spirit continues in them'—'down to the grave' (p 567)—they can still make serious mistakes and act against God's will. So they need *a standard by which to test their free decisions,* to 'pattern and regulate their entire life' (pp 479,480). Therefore Christians need to listen very closely to God's will in the ten commandments and especially in the admonitions of the New Testament.

This is what St Paul means when he writes: 'You were called to be free. But do not use your freedom as an excuse for doing what your selfish nature wants to do. Rather, serve one another in love' (Gal 5:13; see also 1 Pet 2:16). The Galatians *are* free to make their own decisions. But God's command to love, to be selflessly concerned for the welfare of the other person, as Christ was, is to be the standard for them by which they are to measure their free decisions.

In other words, the *Formula of Concord* claims that when we make decisions as Christians we need a standard and a guideline. We need God's commands to prevent us from falling back and becoming slaves of our selfish nature again.

Hard and fast rules for Christians?

Does that mean that there are hard and fast rules which a Christian must obey after all? The answer is no!

We misuse the Bible when we treat its exhortations as a detailed recipe for life which we follow out of slavish fear rather than in love and trust. 'No longer do we serve in the old way of a written law', says St Paul, 'but in the new way of the Spirit' (Rom 7:6 TEV). And Luther follows him when he writes: 'See to it, therefore, that you do not make a Moses out of Christ, or a book of laws and doctrines out of the Gospel' (*Luther's Works* 35,360). Standards and guidelines are fine. But rules which we obey out of a sense of duty put us back under the law. And we know what the law does!

The guidelines of the New Testament are meant to give Christians a 'mirror' of God's will, as the *Formula of Concord* reminds us (p 564). They give us a vision of what God's new world is like. They are like stage directions for a play. To be faithful to the playwright's intention, producer, actors and actresses need to follow the stage directions. But the details of interpretation are left to their creative freedom. They cannot be prescribed.

The command to love

What is the secret of the New Testament guidelines? Strangely, *the Formula of Concord* does not answer that question. But whoever reads the New Testament carefully soon discovers that Jesus expected his followers to make their daily decisions not according to detailed regulations but according to the standard of *love.* In Matthew 22:34–40 Jesus refuses to name one law of God which is more important than any other. Instead, he names the *inner point* of *every* Christian action: love God and love your neighbour.

True, that is a command. It is God's will. But it is not just another law. Strictly speaking, you cannot *command* love. For love is a gift of the gospel. The 'command' explains how every person who lives in Christ *will* act. And therefore the command to love is God's challenge to us *not* to live by fixed rules, which do not involve our heart, but to live and act as Christ did. If Christ gives you the power to love with his love, you *are* doing what God wants (Rom 13:8–10; Gal 5:14; 6:2). My decisions are made in freedom. But love is the direction they are to take, and love is their motivation.

Ethics under the gospel

For example, when the fifth commandment says, 'You shall not kill', God does not mean that you can almost kill a person and still be within the bounds of his will. He means that another person's life, reputation, personality and individuality are valuable, and you should treat that person with the same love with which Christ treated you. Christians do not refrain from committing adultery or stealing or killing or spreading false rumours merely because there is a commandment which says they mustn't. They do so because Christ's love is active in them. But if they disregard the standard of love and do as they please, the law comes with all its threatening force and accuses them so that once more they seek Christ's forgiveness and a fresh start.

Whenever St Paul gives reasons why Christians should act in a certain way he does not appeal to God's law. He refers to the gospel. His commands simply *apply* the gospel to everyday life. He does not say: Wives, submit to your husbands because that is God's law. He says: Do so because you are Christians (Col 3:18, see also 3:12). And in case anyone still sees this as a law discriminating against wives, he adds: 'Husbands, love your wives and do not be harsh with them' (Col 3:19 TEV). Do not run your marriage by rules, but by God's love. In fact, Ephesians 5:21 even goes as far as to say, 'Give way to *each other* out of the respect you have for Christ'. That is how radically the gospel can affect a marriage even in a society like St Paul's, in which the wife was commonly regarded as little better than a chattel.

Christian ethics are based on the gospel, not on the law. As the *Formula of Concord* puts it: 'These works are, strictly speaking, not works of the law but works and fruits of the Spirit' (p 566,567). It is Luther who points out the consequences: 'You should break all the laws rather than to see your brother suffer want or affliction' (*Luther's Works* 51,106). Why? Because no law can guarantee that we will act as Christ did. Only his love in us can do that, because his love goes beyond the call of duty.

No detailed recipes

Because the New Testament is not a detailed recipe for life, it is often easier to describe what Christians will avoid than to say exactly how they will act in every situation. St Paul in Galatians 5:16–25 has no difficulty in detailing the actions of the selfish nature which the Galatians are to avoid. They 'are obvious' (5:19). But when it comes to describing the life of the Spirit, he no longer speaks of obvious actions but of the '*fruit* of the Spirit' (5:22). A detailed recipe cannot be provided for life in the Spirit. But the Spirit does give a guide to the direction this life will take: 'love, joy, peace, patience, kindness, generosity, faithfulness, gentleness, and self-control' (5:22,23). No details here! A standard and a goal for your freedom—with love heading the list!

Christians living by the power of the Spirit are given the freedom to put these guidelines into practice. But they do so under the guidance of God's word. They do not, as the *Formula of Concord* shows, 'set up a self-elected service of God without his Word and command' (p 567). For Christians, who are not only saints but also sinners, have good reason to ask whether it is God's voice they are listening to or their own.

But even then, there are many situations where we have no clear command and where God's word is silent. As a mother of small children, should I take a job or not? How am I to decide on my life's partner? How much of my pay packet should I use for myself and how much should I devote to the work of the church or to alleviate need? Have I the right to buy luxuries for my own pleasure? Should I change my job? How deeply should I involve myself in church work when my family feels neglected?

There are other thorny questions too. Should every conceivable medical measure be employed on a patient when from a medical point of view it will merely prolong the process of dying? Is more than palliative care warranted in this situation? How should a woman act when told after prenatal tests that the child she is expecting will be severely disabled?

The Bible gives us no direct answers to those questions, and in dealing with them we will have to consider not just individual scriptural texts but also general principles and theological insights gleaned from the Bible. But there is one clear command of God: I am to act in love for God and my neighbour. I may be utterly confused about the direction that love is to take. I may need Christian counselling. I will need to speak to God about the decision in prayer. But at some point I will have to make a decision—in faith, remembering that at every moment of my life I live by God's forgiveness.

For example, the young mother will have to ask whether her Christian concern for her children's welfare may not demand the sacrifice of her need for self-fulfilment in a job. Maybe her job is more important to her than her husband's to him, and he will care for the children. Maybe a compromise is possible, part-time work, providing her with the satisfaction and motivation she needs to devote the rest of her time more happily to her children. Wife and husband may need to struggle to find a solution acceptable to both. Maybe her need for personal fulfilment requires a sacrifice of love on his part. Maybe both will need to take a close look at their motivation for working and for having children. Love of God and the neighbour requires all the imagination and creativity of the gospel. Recipes are useless here.

Christian social responsibility

More difficult still is the question of God's will in the area of social responsibility. Society has changed so much since the time of the New Testament that we are confronted with problems today which the writers of the time never had to face. Christians who see the New Testament as a rule book will not have much reason to concern themselves with modern social questions. They will live as though they were in the first century—which is understandably rather difficult to do. Naturally, the New Testament deals with the problems which faced the society of its own time. It applies the command to love to the society it knows, and we are to do the same in ours.

For example, in the first century the relief of poverty was the responsibility of individuals or of local congregations. Because nobody knew what caused large-scale poverty or how to solve it, the economic system itself was simply accepted as a fact of life. However, Christ's command to love clearly meant that the well-to-do should share with the poor. 'Rich people who see a brother or a sister in need, yet close their hearts against them, cannot claim that they love God' (1 John 3:17 TEV; see also Matt 25:31–46; 2 Cor 8 and 9).

But today we understand the economic system which causes rich nations to multiply wealth at the expense of the poorer nations. For example, the poor nations often lack the sophisticated technology of the rich nations, and so cannot compete on world markets unless they sell their inferior products at ridiculously low prices. So the rich get richer and the poor get poorer. There are other factors of course which contribute to poverty, such as droughts, civil warfare—and the fact that industries are often in the hands of overseas owners. We know today that poverty in the Third World cannot be relieved permanently by direct aid, as vital as this continues to be. We also need to implement long-range schemes which change the system causing poverty.

Creative application of the gospel

Do the New Testament commands apply here? The command to love remains central. But beyond that, a Christian will need to listen very closely to the way the New Testament writers apply that command in their own setting. Their admonitions make it clear for all time and for all people that wealth is not given to us for our private enjoyment, but in order to give us the opportunity of practising Christian love (2 Cor 9:6–15; Luke 3:11; 6:30).

But Christian individuals and groups still need to ask how they can best put these admonitions and general principles into practice, in the light of our economic insights today. In addition to direct aid, how can we help to change the system which causes poverty in two-thirds of the world?

In other words, while the Holy Spirit uses the commands of God's word

> to instruct the regenerate out of it and to show and indicate to them . . . what the acceptable will of God is (Rom 12:2) and in what good works, which God has prepared beforehand, they should walk (Eph 2:10)

and

> also admonishes them to do these, (p 566)

in faith and love we often have to decide *how* to apply God's commands in concrete situations.

Making difficult decisions

Think of that woman facing the birth of a severely disabled child. How will she and her partner decide what to do as Christians? Let's hope that they will consider that a child is a gift of God. Let's hope that they will seek out and speak to couples who themselves have disabled children. Let's hope that they will seek expert Christian counselling. Will their love be strong enough to cope with the extra pressures of caring for a disabled child? Will their love perhaps even be enriched by such a child? What sacrifices will it involve? What back-up services are available in the larger family and in the community? How will the couple arrange their own lives and other responsibilities they have around the life of the child?

These are questions to agonise over. But one thing is clear. If a couple like this comes to me for counselling, I dare not say to them: You must do this or do that. I dare not put the pressure of the law on them. How are they to practise Christian love under pressure? And what if, after all the agonising and the counselling, they decide they *cannot* go ahead with the birth? Dare I judge them, if during the prior counselling they have considered all aspects in faith and love? Dare I condemn them? I may disagree with their decision, but I dare not give *them* up. I can only commit them to God's love and care—and the forgiveness which I need as much as they do.

It can indeed be very difficult to decide *how* to apply God's commands in concrete situations today. I wonder whether the *Formula of Concord*, while establishing the principles, did not underestimate the difficulties of decision making in the ethical area.

Be that as it may, people who expect the Bible to give them a set of instructions which they follow blindly and mechanically are living under the law. They will never practise Christian love with their whole heart, soul, mind and strength. For that kind of love is possible only under the gospel. When we live under the law we soon start looking around for loopholes which can give us an excuse for not acting in love as Christians. But the gospel of love involves everything we do, say or think.

The joy of life under the gospel

Therefore the ten commandments and the commands of the New Testament are not really 'law' at all in this case. They are a signpost or compass indicating how we can live out the gospel in practice. They do not say, do this—or else. They say, this is the kind of way you can act in love. They cannot condemn us, for we live under the gospel. They help us to recognise the joy of living under the gospel by the Spirit, and they want to encourage us to live that life for all it's worth! They hold up to accepted sinners all the opportunities available to them in their Christian lives of action. They are a blueprint of the way God wants to use us as his instruments of changing the world. As sinners *we* cannot create that world, as some people today believe. But we are encouraged by the New Testament admonitions to let the Spirit make it visible through our words and actions. The admonitions of Ephesians 4:25–32 are examples of how God's new world begins to take shape through a Christian.

God's commands and admonitions are therefore not a law with conditions. The commands of the New Testament do not say to Christians: *If* you do all this you will be a real Christian who lives by the Spirit. The holiness movements in the church like to think that way. Rather, the New Testament commands say: You already are a Christian who lives by the Spirit, through the preaching of the gospel and through the sacraments. And now this is what your exciting life in the Spirit looks like. Go to it! Walk in the Spirit! Step in line with the Spirit (Gal 5:25)!

Law for the self-secure and lazy

A Christian has freedom in the gospel. But this is not a blank cheque for us to treat God's will lightly or frivolously. Because Christians are still sinners they can get 'lazy, negligent, and recalcitrant'. This is a timely reminder from the *Formula of Concord* (p 566). Indeed, Christians definitely need not only the 'warning and threatening of the law, but frequently the punishment of the law as well', to arouse them 'so that they follow the Spirit of God' (p 565).

This does not mean that whenever we see members of the church doing something which is obviously wrong we should 'throw the book at them'. Rather, we should try to win them over 'in a spirit of gentleness' (Gal 6:1). Why? Because God does not deal with *us* according to the rules either (John 8:3–11)! At the same time we should remember that when the *Formula of Concord* speaks of 'lazy, negligent' Christians it is not necessarily speaking of those who are not as involved in the local womens or youth group as we may be. They may be fulfilling the command to love in quite another area, which we know nothing about. There is no place in the church for pressuring people!

Comfort of the gospel

But there is still hope for those who have acted against the command of love—and which Christian doesn't?

> As often . . . as Christians trip, they are rebuked through the Spirit of God out of the law. But the same Spirit raises them up again and comforts them

> with the preaching of the holy Gospel. (p 566)

To those who are dejected and downcast 'the dear Jesus can never be portrayed sweetly enough' (*Luther's Works* 47,111). And sinners can take comfort from the fact that one day they will 'see God face to face' and 'will do his will spontaneously . . . and with sheer joy, and will rejoice therein for ever' (*Book of Concord,* p 568). Once again the gospel has the last word.

CHAPTER 11

Louder than Words

I once saw a film on television which showed one of those stock comic situations. It dealt with the shy young man, hopelessly in love with the girl of his dreams. She loves him too, of course, but wants to be wooed properly. After the usual misunderstandings he finally plucks up courage to declare his heart but has trouble finding the right words. 'Just say it!' the exasperated young lady tells him. So he blurts out the magic words and two hearts meet. Partnership has been cemented by those simple words.

Of course, the young couple will soon discover that other comic situations will arise—and some that are not at all comical—unless they continue to share their thoughts and feelings in words. Words are one of the ways in which we express and cultivate friendship and fellowship.

Words make friends

This is also the way God makes friends with us—by speaking words of love, comfort and forgiveness. St John calls Jesus 'the Word' (John 1:1,14), for even the sheer presence of Jesus, as well as his words and actions, is a statement of God's love for us. The preaching of the gospel of Jesus Christ plays such a central part in our worship services because through these words God makes friends with us and draws us into fellowship with himself. And once God has spoken to us, we can speak to him too in prayer and praise.

Relationships thrive only when people communicate with one another. We have many ways of communicating and showing friendship, even without words. One of the first things we do when we make new friends is invite them to dinner. People who share a meal together have a special bond of fellowship with one another. A shared meal can speak the truth of friendship more loudly than words.

Friendship without words

This was particularly true in Jesus' time. Table fellowship was an expression of deepest friendship. Whoever ate a meal together belonged together. That is why the decent-thinking people, who took God's laws seriously, were deeply shocked and offended when Jesus sat down to dinner with those who openly flouted God's laws (Mark 2:15–17; Luke 15:2; 19:7). By having dinner with them Jesus seemed to be saying, 'You don't have to obey God's laws to have fellowship with him'. And of course that is exactly what Jesus *was* saying! When he sat down to eat with bad people, it was virtually a public statement that his Father had already accepted them as they were. Jesus' actions spoke the truth more loudly than words.

Wherever Jesus enters into fellowship with sinners, whether it's at a meal—or on the cross—God's forgiveness is already taking place, even if it is not stated in so many words. There is nothing the sinners have to do first; they can simply bask in God's friendship. That is the secret meaning of Luke 7:36–50 too. A woman who has made a mess of her life is given a place in God's heart without a word being spoken. You can tell that she has already been forgiven by the love she shows Jesus and by her tears of joy (Luke 7:47).

Jesus gives God's friendship

Apparently, or so this story suggests, you need only be where Jesus is and look to him and you already have God's friendship. You already belong. And so you already are forgiven. All you can do is be there and be happy in his friendship.

Nowhere is this stated more clearly than in Article VII of the *Formula of Concord* on *The Holy Supper of Christ*:

> We believe, teach, and confess that no genuine believer, no matter how weak he may be . . . will receive the Holy Supper to his condemnation, for Christ instituted this Supper particularly for Christians who are weak in faith but repentant, to comfort them and to strengthen their weak faith. (p 484) This most venerable sacrament was instituted and ordained primarily for communicants like this, as Christ says, 'Come unto me, all who labor and are heavy laden, and I will give you rest' (Matt 11:28). (p 582)

When the Lord's supper is celebrated and we share a simple meal of bread and wine, Jesus Christ, the crucified, risen and ascended Lord, shares himself fully with us by giving us his body and blood 'in, with and under' the bread and wine (pp 575,576). And what happens is what always happens when Jesus gives himself to weak, sinful people: they are reassured that they already are God's friends. They do not have to win his friendship; they merely have to be there and enjoy it.

God's friendship means me

The Lord's supper therefore speaks the gospel more loudly than words. Words can be misunderstood. Even when pastors preach the gospel loudly and clearly, there are always the timid hearers who say to themselves: 'That cannot mean me. I'm not yet good enough. My faith is not yet strong enough.' They still think God makes conditions which they must fulfil before he can call them his friends. Instead of hearing the parable of the two debtors (Luke 7:41,42) in the way Christ meant it—your debts to God, big and small, have already been cancelled—they hear it as though it says, Your debts to God will be cancelled—if you tell him how sorry you are and if you really feel bad about it.

But Jesus says, 'I *have* called you friends' (John 15:15), and he is so eager that the gospel of God's unconditional friendship and love really gets through to us that he simply gives himself to us, body and blood, in his supper. Here there can be no doubt that God's friendship is for me and means me. When I come to the Lord's table and receive him in the sacrament I am told that he receives me as I am. No matter how weak my faith and life, when the pastor gives the bread and the cup and says 'given *for you* . . . shed *for you*', there can be no doubt in my mind that I am included among God's friends. Maybe I don't hear God speaking to me through the preaching of the gospel. But because Jesus Christ is fully present in the Lord's supper I can nevertheless 'taste and see that the LORD is good!' (Ps 34:8). What a 'comfort for all sorrowing hearts' (p 577)!

Fellowship with Christ

The Lord's supper, as the *Formula of Concord* stresses, is therefore 'a true bond and union of Christians with Christ their head' (p 577). When he ascended into heaven he did not leave us alone but comes to be as close to us as he was to the disciples. Luther says Christ wants to be 'just as near to us physically as he was to them' (*Luther's Works* 37,94). We are given the actual presence of his crucified and risen body until the day he returns (1 Cor 11:26). Again and again he reassures us: you belong, you are accepted!

Fellowship with one another

At the Lord's table Christians are also united with one another. Because Christ comes with his presence and makes us God's friends we belong together, much like people around a dinner table. All differences between us are wiped out—by Christ. We are all forgiven sinners.

Christians who are engaged in private warfare need to remember that. When they share Christ's body and blood with others they are confessing that their differences of opinion do not divide them. They are publicly stating—more loudly than words—that they have been made friends. And so the *Formula of Concord* refers to 'a true bond and union of Christians . . . with one another' in the sacrament of the altar (p 577), echoing 1 Corinthians 10:16,17. Christians who share Christ's presence have every reason to solve their differences.

This also applies to the way we treat visitors to our services, or those church members we rarely see. When they attend the Lord's supper they are welcomed by Christ as his friends. How can we then think of them as 'strangers' and leave them to stand on their own after worship, when they are Christ's friends, just as we are? The same is true of refugees from other countries and people of other races communing with us. We will remember Ephesians 2:13,19:

> But now in Christ Jesus you who once were far off have been brought near by the blood of Christ . . . So then you are no longer strangers and aliens, but you are citizens with the saints and also members of the household of God.

The *Formula of Concord* makes it clear that at the Lord's table we are even united in fellowship with those to whom we do not *feel* close! For what is important is not what we feel but the fact that Christ is really present and breaks down the barriers between us.

Calvin and the Lord's supper

One of the most bitter battles fought in the Reformation period revolved around this question of Christ's real presence in the sacrament. Even reformers like Ulrich Zwingli and John Calvin, who were delighted with Luther's rediscovery of the gospel, parted company with him on the understanding of the Lord's supper.

According to the New Testament records, Jesus said that the

bread and wine in his supper *is* his body and blood, but Calvin could not accept that Jesus meant it just like that. Christ's body is now in heaven, Calvin said; how can a human body be in more than one place at a time? And so he claimed that at holy communion everyone receives only bread and wine. He explained that truly pious Christians are inspired by the sacred meal to rise up in faith to heaven, where Christ is, and thus to feed on his body and blood there. Our faith must rise up to heaven first; only then, he said, can we have full fellowship with Christ. His presence is not available to unbelievers.

The gospel at stake

There are those today who think that views like Calvin's do not matter. Like Melanchthon they prefer to look for a compromise for the sake of outer unity. These people overlook that the truth and reliability of the gospel of God's free forgiveness without conditions is at stake here. Can I be sure that Christ comes to me in the Lord's supper with his full presence to tell me that I am already accepted in spite of my weak faith? Or does he make friends with me only *if* my faith is strong? Can I be certain of God's love, or is there an element of doubt?

The writers of the *Formula of Concord* have no other wish than to let the voice of the gospel be heard clearly. How can it be heard clearly when there are those who claim that Christ gives me his body and blood only if I rise up in faith to receive him? Can I be certain of Christ's loving presence, forgiveness, life and salvation only if I am certain of my faith? How can I ever know whether I believe enough? How can I ever be sure that I really meet Christ? Lutherans felt that Calvin's view could lead to endless uncertainty, even fear. Who could dare to go to the Lord's table unless they were a hundred per cent certain of their faith?

No conditions!

There are not many Christians today who still share all the details of Calvin's view. But there are still those who like to make conditions for us to receive Christ's true body and blood: if you really concentrate during the confession of sins the Lord's supper will benefit you; if you really feel his nearness you can be sure that Christ has accepted you as his friend; if you are certain of your faith and really feel bad about your sins you are worthy to attend the Lord's Supper. Those are ifs of the law! They have nothing to do with the gospel proclaimed in Christ's supper.

Perhaps we ought to celebrate holy communion occasionally without confessing our sins first—just to make it plain that the confession of sins is not a necessary condition for receiving Christ's friendship! We can confess our sins without going to communion—but we can also go to communion without having confessed our sins, even if it may be helpful to do so as a rule. Luther said confession is to be 'a voluntary matter' (*Luther's Large Catechism*, p 206).

The *Formula of Concord* is so eager to stress that there are no conditions for receiving Christ's friendship in holy communion, because Christ's friendship is meant precisely for those who are so weak and sinful that they *cannot* fulfil any conditions (p 582). The Formula quotes what Jesus said: 'Those who are well have no need of a physician, but those who are sick . . . For I have come to call not righteous but sinners' (Matt 9,12,13; see p 582). If you are dangerously ill you need a doctor's presence and care. You are too weak to do anything for yourself, even too weak to have real faith in the doctor's ability to cure you. In his supper, Jesus first comes to sick people with all his loving presence and care and attention. Whether we feel it or not, whether we believe it or not, he is there saying, 'You belong to me; I am making you well'. And only then can we believe. Luther rightly said that we should not dare 'to give God something in the sacrament, when it is he who in it gives us all things' (*Luther's Works* 36,98). We have nothing to offer Christ which can impress him, neither our feelings nor our repentance, not even the faith of our hearts. His presence does not depend on anything we do or feel. 'It is not our faith which makes the sacrament, but solely the Word and institution of our almighty God and Saviour, Jesus Christ' (*Book of Concord*, p 585).

Comfort for weak sinners

Article VII is a loud proclamation of the gospel contained in the Lord's supper. It wants to give comfort and reassurance to the weak and uncertain. Christ is truly present in the sacrament as he was when he walked the earth. And he comes with the same love and forgiveness as he did then, even to those who reject him (pp 483,484,573,580,581). They may refuse his friendship and forgiveness (unbelief); but he is there. Weak Christians who are uncertain of their faith but look to him for help can take heart. For there are no conditions to receive his life and love.

> Christ doesn't say: 'If you believe or deserve it, you have my body and blood', but rather: 'Take, eat and drink; this is my body and blood'. (*Luther's Large Catechism*, p 190, quoted by the *Formula of Concord*, p 573)

There can be some doubt about the strength of my faith. There can be no doubt about his presence in the supper, body and blood. 'Here God only gives and he requires nothing . . . We need merely accept and receive his gift. It is literally placed into our mouth' (Edmund Schlink).

'Genuine faith', 'living faith' (p 484) is simply to know: Christ is really there for me! It is not a condition.

Is 'worthiness' a condition?

But aren't there conditions after all, even for Lutherans? Don't we have to be 'worthy' to receive the benefits of Christ's body and blood? Doesn't the *Formula of Concord* echo St Paul (1 Cor 11:27-29) when it says that those 'who go to this sacrament without true contrition and sorrow for their sins, without true faith . . . burden themselves with judgment' (p 582)?

There has often been terrible uncertainty here. Many people still believe that they must *feel* they are sinners to be 'worthy'. They believe that ideally they should spend long, bitter hours of soul-searching to qualify themselves to receive Christ's forgiveness. They are actually afraid of meeting Christ personally instead of looking forward to it. And so they commune rarely or stay away altogether.

Worthiness is hunger for Christ

How tragically they misunderstand the gospel! They should listen to what Luther says in his *Large Catechism*:

> But if you say: 'What if I feel that I'm not ready?', my answer is . . . People like this should learn that . . . this sacrament of ours is not based on what we deserve . . . We come as poor, miserable people, and precisely because we don't deserve anything. (*Luther's Large Catechism*, pp 198–200)

Nor does the *Formula of Concord* say that poor, anxious, confused Christians are unworthy. On the contrary!

> True and worthy communicants . . . are those timid, perturbed Christians, weak in faith . . . who consider themselves unworthy of this noble treasure. (p 582)

> No genuine believer, no matter how weak he may be . . . will receive the Holy Supper to his condemnation, for Christ instituted this Supper particularly for Christians who are weak in faith, but repentant, to comfort them and to strengthen their weak faith. (p 484)

What could be clearer than that? True and worthy communicants are like the sinners of the New Testament who made a mess of their lives and badly needed help—and Jesus came to them and made friends with them.

People who are hungry long to eat. Worthiness for the Lord's supper is simply a hunger for Christ and his forgiving presence. He longs to feed all those who are hungry and weak in faith.

Feelings do not make us worthy

It is certainly not the case that we must *feel hungry* or *feel sorry* for our sins in order to eat at his table. There are no conditions. How could we ever know whether we felt sorry enough? Yet many Christians still try to produce feelings of unworthiness and sorrow to show God that they are worthy and deserve his friendship. They do so because they feel it is expected of them. The *Formula of Concord* reminds us that 'worthiness consists not at all in our own virtues or in our internal and external preparations' (p 484).

Jesus sat at table with sinners. That spoke the gospel more loudly than words. The only person who really knows me—who sees all my actions and all my failures, my thoughts, wishes and desires—invites me to his table without conditions, to come as I am with all my failures and doubts. I do not have to be dressed in a certain way or be in a certain frame of mind. He does not judge me by my clothes and is not impressed by my solemn, downcast eyes. He is interested only in the emptiness inside me, which he is longing to fill with his presence. Of course I will examine my life (1 Cor 11:28). How could any Christian preparing to meet the Son of God not do so? Of course I will need to know that he is truly present. But he does not accept me on the strength of my repentance, or my faith, or my hunger, or my understanding of the 'doctrine of the real presence'. 'Worthiness does not consist in the weakness or certainty of faith, be it greater or smaller, but solely in the merits of Christ' (p 582, see also p 484). All he asks of me is to be ready to receive his friendship.

Therefore, a confused Christian who comes to the altar

expecting and hoping to receive help from Christ personally and who understands only enough to realise that here in this bread and wine is someone who can help, dare not be refused the sacrament. People like this must be welcomed with open arms. For they receive Christ's body and blood as it is intended—in faith. And there we see the gospel—spoken more loudly than words.

Who is unworthy?

True, 'unworthy and godless hypocrites' (p 580) should stay away, for they meet Christ here personally too—as judge. Who are they?

The unworthy are those who take this meal for granted (1 Cor 11:21). Unworthy are those who refuse to admit that they are hungry and need Christ's presence (pp 484,582). Unworthy are those who regard themselves as such good Christians that they see no need for the gift of Christ's body and blood and treat it lightly (1 Cor 11:29). Unworthy are those who believe they have earned the right to receive Christ's presence because they are Christians (or Lutherans), or because they feel truly sorry for their sins, or because they hold the right doctrines, or because they are kind to others. Unworthy are those who are dead certain of their faith and good life—they are really dead! Unworthy are those who have no intention of changing their lives since they are quite happy with the way they are (p 582). Unworthy are those who have no regard for their sisters and brothers (1 Cor 11:18–22). Unworthy are those who think they are worthy!

And if any of these categories fit you *and you want Christ's help*, you know where to go! He is waiting for you with his body and blood to 'make you strong in body and soul to life eternal' (*The Service—Alternative Form*).

The unity we seek

Article VII of the *Formula of Concord* was originally directed at the Calvinists and their Lutheran sympathisers. Today the situation has changed. For some time the Lutheran and Reformed churches in Europe have struggled for unity in their teaching on the Lord's supper. If this is the sacrament of fellowship and Christ welcomes all those who seek his help, we have every reason to try to remove the barriers that separate us. Considerable agreement has been reached. One statement which has been accepted by seventy-seven European churches, the Leuenberg Concord (1973), says that 'Christ gives himself *unconditionally* to all who receive the bread and wine'. Christ's presence does not depend on what we do or feel! In 1994, these churches even agreed that 'when we eat the bread and drink the wine we receive a share in the unique sacrifice of Jesus Christ, in his body and blood, given up for us all'. Lutherans have every reason to rejoice at statements like these. But why is there still some hesitancy to state clearly that when we receive the bread and the wine we actually receive Christ's true body and blood?

Witness to the gospel

The *Formula of Concord* is a permanent witness to the gospel. God doesn't expect anything of us. He simply gives. We can only receive. It is he who acts in the Lord's supper, not we. He makes us his friends so that we can belong to him. The Lord's supper says: Here is the gift of Christ's full presence—for you! Here is the gospel—louder than words!

CHAPTER 12

And There's No Other God

One of the first two people to reach the summit of Mount Everest, Sir Edmund Hillary, when asked why he did it, is said to have replied, 'Simply because it's there!' Similar motives no doubt originally inspired the sophisticated space research programs of Americans, Russians and Europeans. There are problems and challenges which fascinate us and which require all our energies and passions to find a solution to.

Human challenges

That is part of what it means to be human. Athletes train and compete to the very limits of endurance just to prove that a long-standing record can be broken. Scientists may work around the clock to find the answer to a question. A computer freak will brood for long hours to develop new software. We are challenged to find solutions to problems nearly every day.

Yet, surprisingly, none of these challenges fully involve us. When we have solved them our life goes on much as before. We may have discovered new insights and new ways of doing things. We may have a sense of real achievement and pride. But inside we are really no different from what we were before.

Vital questions

However, there are questions which touch on our whole existence. They apply to our deepest needs. We know that we must find answers. The problem does not just fascinate us or challenge us; we sense that our whole life and happiness—and that of others too—depends on finding the right answers.

Everyone has questions like this: What am I here for? No two people on earth are identical; what makes me special? What is the goal of my life? Is there more to life than the fight for survival or the struggle for success? Young people may ask these questions as they begin to think of their future. Elderly people may ask them as they look back and wonder what all their efforts and sacrifices were for.

Or there are other questions: How do I get rid of my worries? Where can I get inner peace? How do I learn to deal with my failures and sense of guilt? How do I find happiness? Who really cares about me? What is the meaning of a life which ends in death? What is the meaning of a world where evil, greed and brutality seem to win out? And finally the really big questions: Why do people suffer? Is there a God? Is he good?

These are questions we have to struggle with. Like other questions they pose a challenge to us. But unlike the other challenges confronting us every day they cannot be solved just by thinking about them hard enough. And they involve us fully in everything we are and do.

Shelving questions

Of course, you can shelve those questions and stumble through life, trying to take things as they come. God knows there is enough to do each day. There is a load of work waiting for you each morning. The house payments have to be made. The children want a swimming pool this summer. The supermarket down the road has a special on saunas. The shopping has to be done, a group of friends is coming over for dinner on Friday night, and there is a wine-tasting on at a small exclusive winery on Saturday. Where will you find time to face the big questions? Who knows whether they can be answered anyway?

Some who sense these questions and whose lives are more hollow than they care to admit follow Eastern philosophies or religions, read esoteric literature, have their horoscopes drawn up and their handwriting analysed, consult clairvoyants and tarot cards, or dabble in reincarnation, mystical stones or sorcery. What motivates them is their belief that there is another spiritual, astral or ethereal world beyond the senses and that certain methods and practices give access to this supernatural world. There they hope to find answers to their questions on the meaning of this world, to discover physical and spiritual health and to learn how to live a happy, fulfilled life. But when the chips are down, don't the big question marks remain?

One main question

An elderly acquaintance of mine was raised without any real contact with the Christian faith. He found himself facing the big questions as a young man amid the rubble of Germany at the end of the Second World War. They gave him no peace. So he set about looking for answers. He read everything he could lay his hands on, the great thinkers and writers of the ages. Finally he stumbled on the figure of Jesus of Nazareth and began to read the New Testament. And he found that all his questions on the meaning of life boiled down to one main question: *Who was Jesus?* His whole life and existence seemed to hinge on the answer to that question. And he found his answers.

God's answer

The *Formula of Concord* in Article VIII on *The Person of Christ* suggests that he is the answer to all our deep questions. We can know what God is really like. We can know what his intention is for our lives and for our world. We can be certain that the road of life we walk together with Jesus Christ is one full of meaning and purpose (Luke 24:13–35). For he has promised us

> that not only his unveiled deity, which to us poor sinners is like a consuming fire on dry stubble, will be with them, but that he, he, the man who has spoken with them, who has tasted every tribulation in his assumed human nature, and who can therefore sympathize with us as with men and his brethren, he wills to be with us in all our troubles also according to that nature by which he is our brother and we are flesh of his flesh. (p 608)

Because God is a human being and a human being is God in Jesus Christ (p 488) Jesus' answers to our questions are God's answers too. What more could we ask for?

Jesus' claims

Therefore the question 'Who was Jesus?' cannot be avoided by anyone who has real questions. Simply because, whatever else Jesus was and whether he has taken hold of our lives or not, he was quite certainly a human being who once made the astounding claim to have answers for all our deepest questions. These are some of his claims:

- Your sins are forgiven (Mark 2:5,9; Luke 7:48)
- I am with you always (Matt 28:20)
- I will not leave you all alone (John 14:18; see also Mark 14:50)
- Do not let your hearts be troubled; believe in God, believe also in me (John 14:1,27)
- Come to me all you that are weary and are carrying heavy burdens . . . and you will find rest for your souls (Matt 11:28–30)

- I am the light of the world. Whoever follows me will never walk in darkness (John 8:12; 9:5)
- I am the bread of life. Whoever comes to me will never be hungry (John 6:35,51,57,58)
- I am the way, and the truth, and the life. No one comes to the Father except through me (John 14:6)
- I am the resurrection and the life. Those who believe in me, even though they die, will live (John 11:25).

What is Jesus' authority?

In these words and many others Jesus claims to have the only answers to life's real questions. Anyone who stumbles on these claims will ask: What is Jesus' authority for speaking like that? Who is this Jesus who claims that God's love, forgiveness and constant support, yes, God's very life, is available through him?

A noble teacher?

Who *was* Jesus? Some say it doesn't really matter; his insights and teachings are the main thing. They help us to understand a little more of life: love God and love others; behave towards them as you would expect them to behave towards you.

Who was Jesus? A noble teacher with some rather fresh insights on the God of love? The greatest man who ever lived? A person who gave us a goal to strive for? The only human being to live in an authentic, holistic way? The champion of the underprivileged and exploited: women, children, slaves? A young man, a lawyer and a Pharisee come to Jesus with ideas like these. They go away disturbed. Jesus wants their hearts, not just their heads. He wants faith, not insights. He refuses to play the role of a teacher (Mark 10:17–22; Luke 10:25–37; John 3:1–15).

Besides, when you are facing a major crisis in your life you are in no frame of mind for noble thoughts and profound insights. When you have a major problem to solve your world and horizons shrink. Nothing else seems important. You have to find an answer. This is all that counts. When your marriage is on the rocks or your children have turned to drugs or you wake up one fine morning wondering what your life has been all about, you will not get much comfort from being told to model your life on the life of Jesus. When you are in terrible pain or are confronted by the media with some of the appalling misery and brutality in our world, it will not help you much if someone points out that a great moral teacher once said that God is good. When you are weighed down by a sense of guilt and failure, no mere human being, no matter how kind and wise, can take that away from you or talk you out of it.

No, I do not need any more teachings about God and life, nor do I need a model to inspire or imitate. I need someone who can assure me with absolute authority that God's love and support are closer to me than my very breathing. I need a person who can make that love and support *real* for me. I need someone like myself, not a super being, someone who has been through it all and can understand me, someone who does not expect too much of me. I need someone like myself who can love, comfort and forgive with *ultimate* authority, the very authority of God.

Jesus claims to do that. And this is the reason why it is vital that I find out who Jesus is.

'Jesus Christ is Lord'

The first Christians heard those claims too. Overwhelmed by their contact with Jesus, his death and his resurrection, they gave the only answer that fitted all the facts as they had experienced them. This man, Jesus of Nazareth, who made all these claims—this is the Lord! When they said 'Lord', they meant exactly what the Old Testament means when it speaks of the 'LORD God' (Hebrew: *Yahweh*) who revealed himself to Moses (Exod 3:13–15). The first believers preached, confessed and sang, 'Jesus Christ is Lord!' (Acts 2:36; 10:36; Rom 10:9; 1 Cor 12:3; Phil 2:11). Jesus of Nazareth is God himself—on my side and at my side.

Jesus' story at two levels

There are two ways of seeing things or people. We can see them from the outside or from the inside. From the outside, flashing lights at a railway crossing are just red lights. From the 'inside', they are a warning signal. From the outside, a person may appear moody, arrogant and cold. But if we look deeper we may discover that on the inside that person is lonely, insecure and unhappy. On the outside, J S Bach's *St Matthew's Passion* is just a mass of black notes on paper, or beautiful choral music. Seen from the inside, it is one of the most profound expositions of Jesus' person and work outside of the Bible.

These are merely illustrations of the way Jesus confronted the disciples and apostles. His story is at two levels. That may surprise us. We tend to think that when Jesus wept for Lazarus (John 11:35) or cried out to God in loneliness and despair (Matt 27:46) or died on the cross, he was acting as a human being, whereas he acted as God when he performed his miracles or rose from death. We tend to see him sometimes as a human being, sometimes as God.

But the New Testament writers don't see him this way. They see everything Jesus did or said on two levels at once.

Truly human

On one level, from the outside, there is nothing so unusual about Jesus. A child is born of poor people under substandard conditions in a one-horse town somewhere in a forgotten corner of the Roman empire. He grows up as a carpenter's son with four brothers and some sisters (Matt 13:55). He is raised as a Jew and comes to the temple as a boy, not to teach but to learn (Luke 2:41–52). At the age of about thirty he begins his career as a wandering preacher after suffering real temptation in the desert and getting himself baptised. After his baptism he seems aware of a special path ahead of him. He impresses people as a gifted person, a prophet perhaps, certainly a teacher who speaks with unusual authority.

True, he performs miracles. Actually, St John prefers to call them 'signs', for they are not meant to prove anything of themselves. They do not convince everybody (Matt 9:34; Mark 3:6; 6:5,6), and others do miracles too (Matt 12:27). Whenever people ask Jesus to support his claims by performing a miracle, he turns them down flat (Matt 4:5–7; 16:1–4; 27:42; Mark 8:11,12; see also 1 Cor 1:22,23!). He doesn't want to force anyone to believe and he is not out to impress anyone. He wants to win people's love and trust. He is just like us (Heb 2:17). He laughs and cries, is timid and angry. He knows he could weaken on the path he has chosen, and he suffers loneliness, terror and fear of death (Matt 26:36–39; Heb 5:7). He dies. Only a real human being can do all that. And yet those who see no more than that miss the whole point.

Truly divine

For there is another level behind all this—the 'inside story'. What this is the disciples really only discover after the resurrection.

But even before, they sense there is something different about Jesus. He is like a breath of fresh air from another world. He teaches 'as one having authority, and not as the scribes' (Mark 1:22). When he heals an epileptic the people are amazed at his authority (Mark 1:27). He claims that his miracles are different from other miracles (Matt 12:28; 11:2–6; see also Isa 35:3–6). They are meant to lift the curtain and give us a glimpse of what God's world looks like when God is at work in it. But even Jesus' ordinary actions and words have a special ring about them.

The gospels rarely say in so many words that this is God, and nowhere does Jesus say it directly. But even the religious leaders, most of whom are interested only in catching him out, have no doubts about what he is claiming. He says, 'You have heard that it was said to those of ancient times . . . But I say to you . . . ' (Matt 5). What was said to those of ancient times? The ten commandments. *God's* ten commandments! Jesus puts himself on a level here with God! Only a megalomaniac can do that—or Someone else! He says, 'Your sins are forgiven', and the scribes are beside themselves with anger: 'Who can forgive sins but God alone?' (Mark 2:7). Who indeed!

Truly divine and truly human

And then there was the cross. On one level, it seems to be the penalty for blasphemy and a sign of dismal failure. And yet the first believers, under the overwhelming impression of the first Easter, suddenly knew: this 'born failure' was God himself, suffering on our behalf, embracing the whole world in love. On one level, shame and disgrace; on the other, the greatest sign of God's glory *in* the shame and God's power *in* the weakness (1 Cor 1:18–25). On one level, a man chooses to give his life for his friends (John 15:13); on another level, his love is so unerring and constant it includes even the unfeeling hooligans around the cross (Luke 23:24).

The only way the New Testament writers can explain the person of Jesus is to confess that this person, who is just like us, has nevertheless come from another sphere. He is anything but a superman—and yet he has all the majesty and power of God himself.

It took the church hundreds of years of reflection and argument before it could express all these insights in clear terms.

But even the New Testament writers knew: *both* must be confessed together—that Jesus Christ is at the same time truly human and truly divine, as the church formulated it later. Nothing else would fit the facts as they had experienced them. Or as Luther put it later in his Christmas hymn:

> Though greater than the earth and skies,
> yet now in Mary's lap he lies.
>
> ('O Jesus Christ, all praise to Thee')

The mystery of Christ

That is the 'highest mystery' (p 489) confessed by the *Formula of Concord* in Article VIII:

> Christ Jesus is henceforth in *one* person simultaneously true eternal God, born of the Father from eternity, and also a true man, born of the most blessed virgin Mary. (p 592)
>
> A single individual is both the Son of God and the Son of Man. (p 487)
>
> Christ is, and remains to all eternity, God and man in one indivisible person. (p 489)

Certainty of God's goodness

Those who are struggling with the deepest questions of life can begin to breathe freely again when hearing this. For they can be sure that wherever they are confronted by Jesus, God is fully present. Wherever they hear Jesus saying to them, 'God loves you', 'God forgives you', 'God accepts you', 'God stands by you', they can be certain that God himself is saying this. God has come to us as a human being—and this human being is God's way of expressing himself most perfectly (John 1:14; Heb 1:3). There are no human depths God has not experienced with us. There are no human questions God has not asked with us. God exposes himself to the very coldness of death so that we do not have to die that way, but can pass straight into his protecting arms. We can be sure that God is a good God because we can see his loving goodness in Jesus Christ. For this reason alone I can be sure that 'nothing can happen to me . . . that has not first passed his inspection and proved to be for my best welfare' (Helmut Thielicke; see also Rom 8:31–39).

Since Jesus accepts me and promises to be with me, I can rely absolutely on God's love and support too. For in Jesus 'the whole fulness of deity dwells bodily' (Col 2:9), and 'apart from Christ there is no God' (*Luther's Works* 37,56; Book of Concord, p 607). 'We must look at no other God than this incarnate and human God' (*Luther's Works* 26,29).

No other God

This is the whole point of the detailed and rather difficult explanations of the *Formula of Concord* in Article VIII:

> And who may this be?
> Christ Jesus is he.
> He is our great Lord,
> there is no other God.
>
> (Luther, 'A mighty fortress is our God')

That means no more and no less than this: If we want to know who God is and what his attitude to us is we are pointed to this human being, Jesus of Nazareth. If Jesus turns in affection to bad, disobedient, selfish, sick and suffering people then that is exactly what God does.

The *Formula of Concord* had to make this point clearly. Calvin and his Lutheran sympathisers claimed that God is not completely bound to Jesus' human nature. They suggested that God is somehow greater than Jesus Christ.

What a terrible thought! How could we ever be entirely certain of God's attitude to us? Maybe he has some private plan for us which he has not revealed in Jesus! If someone close to me had a bad accident which left him or her crippled for life, I could never be sure whether God in his distant majesty was not punishing that person for a particularly sinful life. Only if God *is* identical with the human being Jesus, and this human being is God, can I be sure that in spite of terrible experiences God is still leading us along the same path of love which was revealed in Jesus Christ. Luther's words here are to the point: 'The real God . . . does not want to be found or grasped anywhere else but in this Christ' (*WA* 21,467,10). The evidence: John 14:8–11 and Colossians 2:9!

God of nature

I would say that most people look for a God apart from Jesus. They point to the beauty of a flower, the grandeur of nature, the order of the universe, the miracle of human conception and birth, the ideas of brilliant thinkers. They speak of the 'God of order and harmony'. But is it really God we meet there? Or only a figment of our imagination and a projection of our hopes?

Besides, how does a God like that help me, a speck of dust in the vast expanses of space? Does a God like that care for me? Is he even aware of me? What happens when I no longer have eyes of wonder for beauty, when I observe the struggle for survival among the species, when I observe how wasteful nature is, when I am overpowered by the crushing weight of misery in the world, when I hear that forty thousand children die *daily* of starvation, when I hear of yet another devastating earthquake with many dead and injured? What good is a God of nature when I am up against it, above all when I discover greed and selfishness in myself? In short, how can I know there is a loving God *in spite of everything I see and experience around me*—and not a terrible, destructive, fathomless being, in whose hands I am just a plaything?

God is Jesus

Luther once said, 'To look for God outside of Jesus is of the devil. It leads to despair . . . or presumptuous arrogance' (*WA* 40 III,337,11). If Jesus is not completely one with God, we will never know whether we have God's friendship or his hatred. 'No God like that for me!' (Luther, *Book of Concord,* p 607).

The *Formula of Concord,* on the basis of texts like Matthew 28:18, Colossians 2:9 and Hebrews 2:7,8, makes a particular point of stressing that God is fully present 'in, with, and through' the human nature of Jesus and there 'manifests and exercises his divine power, glory, and efficacy' (pp 603,604). If there is no God apart from and outside Jesus, then God's own power and majesty is shared by Jesus, and there is *no other* majesty and power! Everything God is, this human being Jesus is too. God has bound his power over life and death to the human being Jesus (p 601)—his full authority, his loving will to release us from sin, fears and worries, his unconditional acceptance of us. Luther says: In Jesus we see God's heart unlocked for us; Jesus is 'a mirror of the Father's heart, and without him we can't see anything but an angry and terrible judge' (*Luther's Large Catechism*, p 125). God *is* Jesus.

Comfort and certainty

What an immense comfort! When you are up against it and can see no meaning to your life, the God of nature and the stars will leave you cold. So will the tarot cards and mystical stones and horoscopes and all the other paraphernalia of superstition. But if someone comes and says in person, '*I* care for you. I share all my authority and power with you in a way that you can grasp it, so that you do not have to be afraid of me. I, your God, allow myself to be strung up for you', then indeed you begin to see meaning in your life. You have direct contact, not with a hidden karma or an unpredictable God, but with the love of a human-thinking Father. And that is the *last* word in your life, even when everything else seems to be against you. If this human being is fully God, you can be sure that God *never* plays tricks on you and *never* acts differently from the way Jesus does—even if you often don't know where many of the pieces of the puzzle of life fit into the total picture.

Here is God at our level, a God who proves his love so conclusively on the cross that he cannot and will not—ever—disregard all our other needs and questions.

God—for me

That is a great comfort for all who are struggling to find meaning in life and are seeking God's goodness. They need only hear Jesus' gospel. They need only receive his human body and blood in the sacrament—and they have a direct line to God's innermost heart and all his power. I see a human being healing, and I know that is the beginning of God's all-powerful attack on all suffering and pain. I see a human being comforting and inviting the worried to place their cares on him, and I know that is the beginning of God's all-powerful attack on worry and anxiety. I see a human being forgiving and accepting the scum of society, and I know that is God's all-powerful help for all guilty consciences. I see a human being dying, and I know that is 'God dead, God's passion, God's blood, God's death' for me (p 599). It is not just anyone who has died instead of me; that would not help me much when I must face God. 'But the Son of God himself has truly . . . died' *for* me (p 595; see also p 488). If God has died for me I share his life. And 'if it is not true that God died for us, but only a man died, we are lost' (p 599, see also p 549).

Danger of missing God

The holiness movements and all Christians looking for special experiences should take careful note of this. Since Jesus is the full revelation of God we are not permitted to look for special experiences, feelings, gifts, signs and revelations in order to get closer to God. Nobody dare claim special insights, even if it be in the name of the Holy Spirit. For then that person will miss God at the only place where his full divine nature has been revealed—down at my level, down among all the dirt, grime, suffering, injustice and pain of my life and of the world.

No, I do not have to become godly, noble and pious to share his life and majesty. The almighty God condescends to come to me—in the simplicity of human words from a pulpit, in the simplicity of ordinary bread and wine at the Lord's supper. *That* is how he comes to accept me. And that is the 'inside story' of Jesus of Nazareth.

CHAPTER 13

Happy Ending?

The ostrich is a strange bird: when confronted by danger it is reputed to bury its head in the sand. A similar habit is often adopted by some people—they like to avoid matters which might cause discomfort.

A child caught doing something improper will valiantly try to change the subject. Marital partners will hide a deep-seated problem from each other and live together superficially, instead of seeking counselling. They cannot face the turmoil that may arise when they admit openly that they have a problem. Patients with tell-tale symptoms sometimes refuse to consult a doctor because they are afraid of what a medical examination may reveal.

Even close relatives of patients with an incurable illness imagine that it is better to hide the truth from them. Don't they realise that in giving patients the 'bliss' of ignorance they may be depriving them of their last chance to discover the bliss of God? Or do they hide the truth from them because they themselves can't face the anguish which they imagine the patients will show if told the truth? Pastors are often frustrated because they are so rarely called on to accompany Christians who are dying. 'Death' is often still a dirty word.

'Hell' a dirty word?

This seems to be true of the idea of hell too. Christians take great pains to avoid the subject. One would have to go a long way to find a church where the subject of hell is preached about—alongside the clear message of God's unconditional offer of life in Jesus Christ. It seems embarrassing to tell people who spend their lives in the pursuit of fun that there may not be a happy ending after all.

Naturally, we are rightly suspicious of the sects which concentrate on painting a vivid picture of the horrors of hell and use the threat of eternal flames and devils with red-hot pincers as a lever to gain fanatical supporters of their cause. You cannot frighten people into heaven. Besides, those gruesome and colourful pictures of hell do sound naive and a little ludicrous at the beginning of a new millennium. So we tend to avoid the subject of hell altogether.

Hell in this life

But even if we are embarrassed to raise the subject of hell, there are plenty of people today who claim that we have imported hell into this life. There are those who will never forget the carefully planned extinction of six million Jews and gypsies or the indescribable suffering of human guineapigs in Auschwitz and other concentration camps under Hitler. Eugen Kogon, a Jewish psychiatrist who spent eight years in such a camp—and by some miracle survived—wrote a book afterwards called *The Theory and Practice of Hell.*

First circle of hell

'Abandon all hope, you who enter here.' Those were the words inscribed over the gates to hell in the *Divine Comedy* of Dante nearly seven hundred years ago, and untold millions in two world wars, in countless wars since and in concentration camps have come to taste the terrible meaning of that motto.

In Alexander Solzhenitsyn's novel, *The First Circle,* dealing with one of the worst periods of oppression in the former Soviet Union, Russian prisoners under Stalin are transferred from the suffering and degradation of a labour camp to Mavrino, a special prison for intellectuals situated in a converted country house on the outskirts of Moscow. They regard their new 'freedom' as heaven. 'No', says Lev Rubin, 'you are in hell, just as before. But you have graduated to its best and highest circle—the first circle' (pp 19,20). At the end of the story, as a group leaves Mavrino for a labour camp with its brutality, humiliation, starvation rations, despair and death, one man says, 'I shouldn't worry about leaving Mavrino . . . It's hell, I tell you!' Nerzhin, one of the characters, replies crisply, 'No, Ilya, it's not hell. *That's* not hell! Where we're going—*that's* hell' (pp 698,699).

Hell for these writers is to have to live a life without meaning and purpose of any kind. Hell is to be cut off from all sympathy and love. Hell is to be without hope. Hell is to be treated without dignity, as though one had no feelings. Hell is to be beaten, tortured, brainwashed and starved—until one's identity is crushed beyond recognition. That's how many today see hell.

How strange it is that Christians often leave it to others to speak of hell in their own way!

Hell is other people

Most of us have no first-hand experience of the 'hell' we read about or see on our television screens. However, the fingers of hell can leave their imprint on our personal experiences too.

In a play first produced in Paris in 1944, Jean Paul Sartre comes to the conclusion that 'hell is other people'. What he means is that people make one another's lives real hell. Instead of love and acceptance, there is bickering and needling. Instead of trust and honesty, there is suspicion and scheming. Instead of care and concern, there is neglect and selfishness. And bit by bit life can lose all meaning and turn sour on us.

A taste of hell now

Who will dare to say that all this is not at least a whiff or a taste of hell already in this life? It is true that the Bible means more than that when it refers to hell. But the experiences of a hell on earth do remind us that we live on the brink of terror and utter God-forsakenness. Perhaps that is something of what is meant in the medieval hymn *Media vita*, which Luther rewrote:

> In the midst of life we are
> quite by death enfolded . . .
>
> In the midst of death, perceive
> How hell's jaws distress us! . . .
>
> In the midst of hell's grim dread
> us our sins are driving . . .
>
> (*WA 35 Supplement*)

Hell is the experience of death's terror in the midst of life. Anyone who can no longer discover any meaning in life and cannot find God's fatherly hand in the midst of pain and despair already has a taste of what hell is.

Hell is separation from God

The *Formula of Concord* in Article IX on *Christ's Descent into Hell* refrains from saying what and where hell is. But Luther, who experienced the bitter struggles of conscience in the face of God's silence, had no doubt that this was hell. Hell, he says, need not be a special 'place':

> Everybody carries his hell with him wherever he may be so long as he feels the final anguish of death and God's anger. (*Luther's Works* 19,75)
>
> A heart that is sick and always conscious of sin is a perpetual hell. (*Luther's Works* 8,52)

In other words, it is not the heat that makes hell what it is. It is the torment of knowing that God is near—but that one is cut off from him all the same. That is the way Jesus describes hell in the parable of the rich man and Lazarus (Luke 16:19–31). 'To have to look at the spring of life without being able to drink from it—that hurts!' (Helmut Thielicke). That is hell.

Is separation from God torment?

It might of course be objected that a vast majority of those today who are cut off from God don't seem to suffer the torments of hell now. On the contrary, isn't it a fact that many who take God for granted and exclude him from their everyday lives are quite happy? It is certainly not much use to suggest to them that their lives are meaningless and empty when they feel quite happy and fulfilled—and sorry for all those churchgoers with hang-ups who waste a beautiful Sunday morning listening to some boring preacher. People who feel this way may be separated from God, but they certainly do not always experience it as hell and torment.

The discovery of hell

Yet as Luke 16:19–31 suggests, people like this are actually on the threshold of hell without being aware of it. You can actually shut God out of your life without realising what you are missing. But the time must certainly come when you will become aware of your emptiness and lostness apart from God, and then all hell can break loose.

This discovery of hell may start with the tragic, apparently meaningless death of a loved one, or with the news that you are incurably ill, or with the disintegration of your family. None of these experiences *need* be a taste of hell. People who have learnt over many years to trust God's love in Jesus Christ may be badly shaken by events like these, but the house of their life is built on a rock, and even the most violent storms will not destroy it. On the other hand, those who believe in God only as a kind of insurance policy against unhappiness will see no meaning in their suffering; the house of their life is built on sand and is toppled by the storms (Matt 7:24–27). They may cry out, Why has God done this to me? How can God be good?—and never find the answers, because they have never really *lived* with God, never pondered his ways, never considered who they are and where they are going. But when tragedy strikes there *are* no quick answers. Where there is no fundamental trust in God, from whose love in Christ nothing can separate us (Rom 8:38,39), there is only silence and anguish, and God seems aeons away. That is hell now.

God calls us lovingly through his word to live with him and share his life of meaning and purpose. Those who refuse to hear that word and make it part of their life are turning their backs on God. At some point—whether in this life or on the day of judgment at the end of time—they will realise that they have missed out on the whole point of their life. They will recognise God as he really is in Jesus Christ—and be excluded from him. That is eternal hell.

Living in fear of hell?

What a sombre thought! Who can escape God's anger? Can we be sure that God has accepted us in Christ? After all, who of us really lives with 'fundamental trust' towards God? Don't we sometimes have a taste of hell even now? Don't we as Christians need to live in fear of the possibility of an eternal hell? Perhaps, after all, *that* is the real reason why we prefer to banish the idea of hell from our thoughts.

In the year 359 the Synod of Sirmium added three Latin words to the Apostles' Creed which are meant to give us an answer to those questions: *descendit ad inferna*—Jesus Christ 'descended into hell'. For centuries it was agreed that this is a message of comfort and hope. But what do these words really mean?

Christ's suffering in hell—for us

John Aepinus, a Lutheran pastor in Hamburg, took up this question in 1549. He suggested that the words, 'he descended into hell', are simply another way of describing the terrible depths of Jesus' suffering and death on our behalf. He wrote:

> I believe that the descent of Christ's soul to hell was a part of Christ's passion, i.e., of the struggles, dangers, anguish, pains and punishments which he

took on himself and bore for our sake. (quoted by F.H.R. Frank)

Many Christians still get much comfort from this view. Even Luther claimed on the basis of Acts 2:27 that St Peter wants us Christians to think of hell 'as the pain of death Christ felt when He died on the cross' (*Luther's Works* 19,75). When Jesus on the cross cried out in terror, 'My God, my God, why have you forsaken me?' (Mark 15:34), he showed that he was 'forsaken by God as one eternally damned' (*Luther's Works* 42,105). What made Jesus' death different from every other horrible death was the fact that he who was closer to God than any other human being experienced the utter depths of God-forsakenness. Jesus was the most tormented and abandoned of all human beings. His death was sheer hell.

Christ shares our hell

Those who take this line say that Jesus suffered the very depths of hell and despair, so that in all the hells we experience, even though they are only the 'first circle' of hell, we can be sure that we are not alone. As Luther put it, 'in that picture your hell is defeated and your uncertain election is made sure' (*Luther's Works* 42,105). Christ is the brother of all lost, lonely, tortured and suffering men and women. He is on their side and at their side in the midst of their anguish. God has entered our hell. I can be ever so low, but God has been lower.

Christ's victory over hell—for us

The *Formula of Concord* in Article IX does not specifically reject this view. It leaves the matter open (*Book of Concord,* p 492). It simply lays the stress on the one point which Aepinus had denied. We can be sure of one thing, the *Formula of Concord* states. When Christ went to hell he

> destroyed hell for all believers, and has redeemed them from the power of death, of the devil, and of the eternal damnation of the hellish jaws. (p 492)

That is the comforting message of the Apostles' Creed when we confess, 'he descended into hell'. A victory has already been won for us! Everything Jesus did from his birth to his ascension he did for us, to defeat anything that could cut us off from God and to bring God's life as closely to us as possible.

No hell for believers

For those who simply clutch at Christ *there is no hell*, there is no death, there is no devil. For them hell, death and devil do not exist! When the *Formula of Concord* makes this bold statement of the gospel and tells us simply to 'cling to the Word' (p 610), the writers were no doubt thinking of texts like Hosea 13:14, Colossians 2:15 and Revelation 1:18. Christ has been through hell and has cleaned it up, as Luther stressed in an Easter sermon of 1533 to which Article IX refers. Hell can hold no final terrors for us! Paul Gerhardt summarises the matter beautifully:

> Defeated, overpowered,
> the prince of hell there lies;
> his deadly raging silenced,
> no more can he arise.
> The Lord now has hell's key,
> he who triumphantly
> the power of death laid low,
> and holds in bonds the foe.
>
> ('Awake my heart, rejoicing')

Therefore—and this is not said lightly—no power can ever separate us from God's love shown in Jesus Christ: no Hiroshima, no Auschwitz, no labour camp, no apparent hell we experience.

Is it by accident that towards the end of his description of the helplessness and terror of the 'first circle' of hell Solzhenitsyn refers to the continued hope of the prisoners with the words: 'Thus Christ in the Garden of Gethsemane, though he knew that he must drink the bitter cup to its dregs, continued to hope and pray' (*The First Circle*, p 691)? To alter an old proverb: Where there's hope there's life—even in the midst of bitter cups!

The comfort of Christ's victory

Hence, no matter how terrible our life and how deep the hell we seem to experience, anyone who can confess, 'He descended into hell', can be absolutely certain that God's love is greater than any hell. 'The darkness and night of hell is outshone by the light of the victory of our Lord Jesus Christ' (Hans-Martin Helbich). Christ's descent into hell gives us 'the comfort that neither hell nor the devil can take us or any believer in Christ captive or harm us' (*Book of Concord*, p 610).

People in pain or suffering from a terminal illness or in

turmoil at God's seeming silence in their lives can take comfort. They can follow Christ without fear wherever he may lead them. For they have the promise that nothing they experience is really hell. Wherever they may find themselves, even if it seems to be hell, God is there, waiting for them with open arms (Ps 139:8), offering them victory. Nothing I experience need be hell as long as I am sure of that. My 'hell' is merely the privilege of sharing in Christ's suffering—and it brings with it the certainty of sharing in his victory!

Our hells have a limit

There is a limit to all our little hells on earth. They are not the final word. Hell's power is broken. 'The glimmer of dawn has begun to break above the fields of death and the places of murder, and also above the little hells of everyday life' (Jürgen Moltmann). We have no need to bury our heads in the sand at the thought of hell. While we are with Christ there *must* be a happy ending.

CHAPTER 14

Free – to Serve the Gospel

People still lay great store by polite behaviour, and unless we return to the jungle they probably always will. What constitutes good manners varies from place to place and age to age, but in all societies human relationships are regulated in some way.

Of course, in each generation there are those who question our standards of polite behaviour. Young people are often critical of accepted traditions which seem to be merely outward forms. They claim that good manners are often only a cover-up for insincerity and hypocrisy and are therefore no more than a hollow shell.

Etiquette and freedom

Most people would agree that a natural and honest approach is best. But there is still a place for good manners. They are certainly not meant to be a veneer, hiding our true feelings. They are forms of behaviour which help us to express our regard and thoughtfulness for others. For instance, it is etiquette not to empty your glass of champagne before the toast has been proposed to the guest of honour. By waiting you show that you are not just there for the drink but for the sake of the person being toasted. It is thoughtless and rude to disregard all guidelines for good manners.

The danger with all guidelines is that they can become hard and fast rules which have no real meaning any more, but which you follow slavishly all the same. Years ago when knives stained easily and were hard to clean, it was important to show your consideration for your hosts by using a fork to divide your roast potato, and not a knife. In an age of stainless steel knives it would be petty to insist on this rule. Really well-mannered people may not always stick to all the 'rules'. They will often decide from case to case for themselves what best serves their relationship with others and shows their consideration.

Church practices not essential

In the church too there are practices and traditions which have been introduced 'for the sake of good order and decorum', as the *Formula of Concord* states in Article X on *Church Usages, Called Adiaphora or Indifferent Things* (p 610, see also p 492). The writers are thinking here of 'ceremonies or church usages' (p 492), and these include all the customs and practices of the church: the liturgy, the church building and everything in it, the pastor's vestments, the liturgical colours, the time at which worship services are held, the kind of music we have, even the structures of church organisation and the forms of church government and administration we employ. Of all these things the *Formula of Concord* states that they are

> neither commanded nor forbidden in the Word of God but have been introduced into the church in the interest of good order and the general welfare. (p 492)

Neither flowers in the church nor the liturgy nor church committees nor even church schools rest on a command by God. Choirs are not God-given nor youth groups nor even synodical conventions. In fact, most of the church's activities which consume so much of our time are not essential in the church. They are simply human customs and are to be treated as such. As with rules of etiquette, what is essential in these 'ceremonies and church usages' is not the outward form we use but what they are meant to express.

Only the gospel is essential

What then *is* essential in the church? Three things only: the preaching of God's word, the celebration of baptism and holy communion (as Christ commanded it, p 584) and the office of the ministry. Anything else we do in the church may be good and useful, but it is not essential. What is essential centres around the gospel of God's love in Jesus Christ and the proclamation of that gospel.

Our relationship to God is created by the preaching of the gospel in word and sacrament, not by our church activities. That relationship does not depend on whether we sit or stand at services, whether we like organ music or not, or whether the pastor wears vestments or shorts. It is not dependent on whether we have a pipe organ, stained-glass windows, or even a proper church building. These may be desirable, but they are not essential. But there can be no church without the gospel. The church can continue to exist without everything else. It can be a tin shed with an upturned packing case for an altar and a battered mug for a chalice—as long as the gospel is preached and the sacraments are administered.

Human traditions do not save

That may upset some Christians. The fact is that people will fight much more passionately over the question of how to decorate the church's Christmas tree than over the question of faith. People who care little about what is preached on a Sunday morning will take to the barricades over a question of ritual or tradition.

But the *Formula of Concord* makes a careful distinction between what is vital in the church and what is not. By confessing this, Lutherans are saying: What is really important in the church is not created by us with our traditions, forms, structures and plans, but by the Holy Spirit through the preaching of the gospel. As Luther stressed, the gospel brings forgiveness, life and salvation; ceremonies and human traditions do not:

> We do not despise ceremonies and works, but we set great store by them; but we despise the false estimate placed upon works in order that no one may think that they are true righteousness. (*Luther's Works* 31,376)

As soon as we regard our church activities and forms as essential we obscure the gospel, which tells us that God has accepted us as we are, without all our activities and church practices.

Non-essentials are important

Why then should we bother with these non-essentials which the *Formula of Concord* calls 'adiaphora'? Why don't we just do as we please in the church?

Non-essentials are a little like good manners. Just as we find outward forms useful in regulating our daily relationships with others, so the church cannot do without practices and customs to help it in carrying out its essential task of proclaiming and living the gospel. You cannot build a house without scaffolding. But you do not build a house for the sake of the scaffolding and you would be stupid to regard your scaffolding as the real thing. In the same way, the non-essentials in the church's life are useful tools which help to build up Christ's body and assist God's people in their task of proclaiming the gospel in word and action. We cannot do without them.

No-one dare take these practices and customs lightly. In many cases they are traditions which have developed in more than a thousand years of the church's experience with the gospel.

Liturgy as a witness to the gospel

For example, our service orders have proved themselves over the centuries as admirable instruments which serve the gospel.

By starting our communion service with a confession and absolution of sins, we are reminded that the starting point of our relationship to God is *his* forgiveness and acceptance, not *our* religious fervour or holy intentions. Only then, when we have been assured of his attitude to us, dare we break out in praise of his glory (in 'Glory to God in the highest'). In the central part of the liturgy we do not concentrate on our own ideas or feelings but listen to God speaking to us through the Bible readings and the gospel of the day. In the sermon God's message is applied to us in our own situation. We respond in faith to that gospel message in four ways: by the confession of our lips in the creed; by the symbols of thanks and love in the offering; by the dedication of our whole lives to God in the offertory; and by our prayers of thanks and intercession 'for the whole people of God in Christ Jesus and for all people according to their needs'. That is how we begin our service of the gospel which will continue in the week ahead. After communing with Christ and one another, the blessing sends us back into our normal everyday life with the assurance of the ongoing presence of Christ, as we continue our divine service of the gospel by being 'little Christs to others', as Luther put it.

The riches of our worship tradition, which we share with Anglicans and Roman Catholics, may be non-essentials. But they can be a powerful witness to the gospel message, a kind of dramatic enactment of the gospel, even when the sermon provides little more than entertaining stories or merely makes moral appeals.

No place in the church for whims

True, the liturgy is a non-essential, and therefore a pastor and congregation could simply decide to alter it or replace it with something else, if they were convinced it would be

> most profitable, beneficial, and salutary for good order, Christian discipline, evangelical decorum, and the edification of the church. (p 612)

But usually this would be an action taken by the whole church body. Otherwise, pastors and congregations would be in danger of constructing something which does not, in fact, serve the full gospel but merely caters for their own needs and whims. It has been rightly pointed out that 'uncared-for liturgy is certain to say anything but the gospel' (Eric Gritsch and Robert Jenson). Proclamation of the gospel is not likely to be very convincing when a do-it-yourself liturgy quietly suggests that God accepts us on the basis of something else!

Traditions can serve the gospel

There are other traditional practices and customs in the church of a more symbolic and artistic nature. They are also tools which help the proclamation of the gospel. Although they too are non-essentials they should not just be dismissed as irrelevant. In each case we must ask: are they effective in promoting the message of God's love and acceptance in Christ? If they are, let's keep them—and make sure they meet accepted standards of artistic taste. If they are not, let's look around for something else.

The power of the gospel, word and sacraments, does not depend on what a pastor wears at a worship service. But the alb and stole is undoubtedly a more festive witness to the joy of the gospel than ordinary street dress. Flowers are not essential in the church, and it is certainly not a crime when someone has forgotten to do them. But who will deny that some of the most glorious products of God's creation (Matt 6:28,29) have their place in the church? Don't they remind us of God's love for us, which creates beauty for us to enjoy? And don't a few living twigs in winter serve the gospel better than bunches of artificial flowers, which may decorate but do not witness?

Church music and hymns are not essentials either. But for two thousand years faith in the gospel message, expressed in music, has given courage and joy to countless Christians: the music and hymns of people like Luther, Paul Gerhardt and Charles Wesley, accompanied on the organ; and the music and songs of today, accompanied by keyboards and electric guitars. Choirs singing Bach and gospel groups singing modern spirituals—all serving the gospel. What a breadth of possibilities here!

Church buildings are non-essentials too. But anyone who worships in a well-designed church, with its focal point on the crucifix at the altar and its effective and artistic use of light, colour and symbolism, will know how it supports the proclamation of the gospel.

Need to understand church practices

Of course, if people no longer understand the meaning of the liturgy and other practices of the church, their worship will soon degenerate into formal habit. And then worshippers may soon get the idea that mere attendance at the liturgy qualifies for God's special approval.

When people do not understand them, church ceremonies become 'useless and foolish spectacles' (p 611), for they no longer serve the gospel but have become an end in themselves. There is a constant need in the Lutheran church for the liturgy and other practices to be explained, so that they do not become a hollow shell.

Traditions are not a 'must'

But while there is no place in the church for individual whims and we always need to consider what is for the good of the whole people of God, church traditions and practices are and remain adiaphora, non-essentials. They were devised by human beings; they did not fall from heaven. They dare not become a 'must' which permits no alternatives. As usual, Luther puts it most simply: 'You ought . . . not make liberty a law' (*Luther's Works* 51,81). A 'beautiful service' may please us, but it does not guarantee God's acceptance of us. Only the clear message of the gospel can do that.

The strict unyielding supporters of church practices, who get so upset when even the slightest detail of long-standing traditions is changed, or even look for support in the Bible for keeping to particular rubrics (ie the 'stage directions' of the liturgy), need to be reminded of that. Traditions and rubrics may be hallowed by time. They are certainly not hallowed by God.

Freedom in non-essentials

Total uniformity in the church is not only dull; it can also develop into legalism. Nor will everything which is right for one church always be right for another. Jesus Christ gave us freedom in these matters. He commands purity of heart and faith in God, not the outward observance of traditions. They do not qualify us for God's acceptance (Matt 15:1–20; see also Gal 5:1; Col 2:8,16; Rom 14). Quoting texts like these, the *Formula of Concord* reminds us that we are free to find the *best* means of serving the gospel.

> We further believe, teach, and confess that the community of God in every place and at every time has the right, authority, and power to change, to reduce, or to increase ceremonies according to its circumstances, as long as it does so without frivolity and offense but in an orderly and appropriate way, as at any time may seem to be most profitable, beneficial, and salutary for good order, Christian discipline, evangelical decorum, and the edification of the church. (p 612)

It may indeed happen that certain aspects of the church's practices no longer mean much to a large number of people and can therefore no longer serve the gospel proclamation efficiently. Many of those outside the church today regard our practices as mumbo jumbo. If we insist on one kind of 'style' in the church, we may be hindering the proclamation of the gospel among the unchurched. But even within the church there are those who do not feel at home with all of our traditions and ceremonies. The complaint that our services are often dull and insipid cannot simply be dismissed out of hand.

Need for variety

Perhaps we need a variety of ceremonies, church rites and alternative service forms so that a greater number of people may discover the gospel in their own 'idiom' or style. Romans 14, quoted by the *Formula of Concord* with obvious approval, certainly suggests that there is plenty of room in the church for variety! A formal liturgical service with Gregorian chanting, pipe organ accompaniment and all the trappings may serve the gospel best for some, while an informal family service with an overhead projector, contemporary music and drama may be a better channel for the gospel for others. What a wealth of spiritual songs has been composed and written over the last twenty-five years or so! Pastors and congregations should consider their 'clientele' more and ask in what way their need for the gospel is being met. We dare not be legalists here! Those who insist on the classical order of service at all times and regard contemporary music or alternative worship styles as 'unsuitable', offend just as much against Article X of the *Formula of Concord* as those who insist that traditional worship is sheer formalism and a barrier to the spontaneous working of the Spirit. God can use all kinds of human traditions to get his gospel through! Our preferences are not decisive; the gospel message is.

Freedom to change church practices

In cases like these the Formula of Concord expects us to use our Christian freedom

> to change such ceremonies according to circumstances, as it may be most profitable and edifying to the community of God. (p 493)

The worship service is not there for us to celebrate our likes and dislikes. It is to be the most effective vehicle of God's message of unconditional love.

Our freedom in non-essentials applies to the whole area of church government too. Church structures, church institutions and church administration are important. But they exist only to serve the gospel message. If they no longer do so, or no longer do so effectively, we have the freedom to replace them with ones that do. At every synodical convention delegates are being challenged to examine their system of administration and organisation. Is this the best way of serving the gospel? Is a system of presidents, districts, church councils, commissions, committees and boards the most effective means of furthering Christ's gospel? Are there alternatives? Are some of the church's districts or dioceses too large, while others are too small? Has the General Convention become too large and unwieldy because of the system of parish representation? Are pastors and congregations too independent in their relationship to the church at large? Whatever the answers to these questions might be, the *Formula of Concord* reminds us that our systems and structures are not God-given. They are there to do a job.

In all non-essentials there is freedom. Here 'there is to be neither commanding nor forbidding', as Luther observes (*Luther's Works* 40,130).

Sacrificing freedom in love

But there are times, as the *Formula of Concord* stresses, when we have to be ready to sacrifice our freedom in non-essentials. Many Christians have not yet discovered this freedom of the Christian. Their weaker faith must be respected out of love.

After all, Christ has accepted the weaker persons as they are, as St Paul explains in Romans 14:13–21 and 1 Corinthians 8:9–13. The *Formula of Concord* states the matter succinctly:

> In this matter all frivolity and offenses are to be avoided, and particularly the weak in faith are to be spared. (p 493)

Of course, the 'weak in faith' are not those who happen to disagree with whatever changes to tradition you are proposing, and it would be unfair of anyone to claim they were 'weak in faith', merely as a tactic to stop reforms. The 'weak in faith' are those who have not understood the freedom of the gospel and whose faith would be threatened if, say, the committee on which they have been serving for the last thirty years or so was to be dissolved in the process of restructuring. Whatever decision was ultimately made, those responsible would have to consider that in non-essentials love is more important than being right.

Freedom or compromise?

There are other times too when the church must be prepared to forgo its freedom in non-essentials. In the sixteenth century, war broke out between the Lutheran princes in Germany and an alliance of Roman Catholic princes. Under the emperor, Charles V, the Roman Catholic forces were superior. Charles wanted the empire united but could not stamp out Lutheranism. So he had a proposal drawn up which allowed Lutherans to continue to worship but virtually suppressed all their teachings. The proposal met with stiff opposition on the part of pastors and congregations. To prevent wholesale persecution, the mild-mannered Melanchthon agreed to reduce Lutheran teachings to the absolute minimum. This Leipzig Interim, as it was called, clearly stated that God accepts us without conditions. But it restored most of the old Roman Catholic practices. Melanchthon claimed that they were non-essentials and that Lutherans were therefore free to accept them. But the strict Lutherans under Matthias Flacius accused him and his supporters of betraying the Lutheran cause. Lutherans were split into two camps.

The *Formula of Concord* deals with this problem in Article X and decides in favour of Flacius:

> We believe, teach, and confess that at a time of confession, as when enemies of the Word of God desire to suppress the pure doctrine of the holy Gospel, the entire community of God . . . [is] obligated to confess openly, not only

> by words but also through . . . deeds and actions, the true doctrine . . . In such a case we should not yield to adversaries even in matters of indifference, nor should we tolerate the imposition of such ceremonies on us by adversaries in order to undermine the genuine worship of God. (p 612; see also p 493)

No freedom to compromise the gospel

In short, Lutherans normally would have the freedom to accept a hierarchical episcopal structure, a liturgy in Latin, Roman Catholic or Anglican or Orthodox vestments, and even special periods of fasting—if they decided that these would best serve the gospel. Melanchthon was right in saying that in themselves these things are non-essentials.

But the picture changes when another church, for which these practices are essential, *demands* them of us, for example as a condition of unity. By following their demands, Lutherans would virtually be saying: Other human practices and traditions are essential *alongside* the preaching of the gospel, when it comes to our relationship with God. We would be asserting that God accepts us not only by his mercy and grace in Jesus Christ but also on the basis of our structure of church government, or the kind of liturgy we use, or the way a pastor is dressed, or whether we give up certain foods several times a year.

To accept non-essentials when they are demanded of us, as the *Formula of Concord* points out, would create the impression that we do not take the gospel and the gospel alone seriously (p 611). It would 'undermine the genuine worship of God' (p 612) and 'suppress the pure doctrine and Christian liberty' (p 613). We would no longer be free to decide what best serves the gospel. Here the *Formula of Concord* is only repeating what St Paul says: 'For freedom Christ has set us free. Stand firm, therefore, and do not submit again to a yoke of slavery' (Gal 5:1).

Non-essentials dare not be made essentials

Nearly all denominations today still differ on questions of church government. Some have a long tradition of bishops and a hierarchical system reaching back to the fourth century or beyond. Others are ruled by elders. Others have a form of government in which local churches have the final say. Others lay great store by a system of presidential democracy. None of these systems presents any great problems to Lutherans, and most of them will be found somewhere in the Lutheran world. In fact, the *Formula of Concord* dismisses all the problems in one sentence:

> We believe, teach, and confess that no church should condemn another because it has fewer or more external ceremonies not commanded by God, as long as there is mutual agreement in doctrine and in all its articles as well as in the right use of the holy sacraments. (p 493)

We are free to accept whichever system serves the gospel best—unless one particular form or another is demanded of us as a condition of unity. Then we must resist—or else we compromise the freedom of the gospel.

The freedom of Lutheranism has been an ecumenical blessing and an ecumenical problem. It is a blessing because we are open to other forms of organisation, ritual, church practices and traditions. It is a problem because most Lutherans will agree that no structure or ritual or tradition is what God 'really' wants. We are wary of obscuring the gospel by legal requirements. We need the freedom to use whatever best serves the gospel. What is essential for unity between Lutherans and other churches is that they can preach the gospel together and agree on how to do it. And that is *all*.

Freedom is a great privilege to be enjoyed. We have the freedom for and the freedom from church traditions. But freedom is also a great responsibility to be guarded. We dare not allow ourselves to be constricted on our one essential task: to point to the love of God in Jesus Christ.

C H A P T E R 1 5

Chosen!

Little children at play are a delight to watch. The simplest household utensil can occupy them for hours on end. Even the most humble object interests them as they explore its possibilities. They seem to take nothing for granted. Everything they discover is new and exciting.

It is like that with many adults too who come to trust Jesus Christ for the first time. They have discovered something new. Their life has fresh meaning and purpose. What we may take for granted they see as a miracle.

The freshness of the gospel

Of course, converts have no monopoly on the freshness of the gospel. You may have grown up a Christian and have taken it more or less for granted. But one day the old well-known texts of the Bible sprang to life. God seemed to be speaking to you personally. It may have been during a serious illness or a time of great sorrow or a personal crisis. You had heard the words before: 'I will be with you; I will not fail you or forsake you' (Josh 1:5); 'Remember, I am with you always' (Matt 28:20); 'Nothing in all creation . . . will ever be able to separate us from the love of God which is ours through Christ Jesus our Lord' (Rom 8:39 TEV). Perhaps one of those passages was your confirmation text. But now it struck you that those words were written for *you*. They had a freshness you had never discovered before. And one by one other texts took on new meaning. You suddenly knew: Nothing can go wrong! God won't let me down! Suddenly your faith had greater meaning.

Why do people believe?

How do people come to discover that the gospel of God's love is fresh and exciting? For one person it is a sudden experience, as it was for St Paul (Acts 9:1–19a; 22:6–16; 26:12–18). For another, like St Peter, it is a slow growth, punctuated by dazzling insights (Mark 8:27–30)—but also by dismal failures (Mark 8:31–33; 14:66–72). Some people are raised by believing parents. Others find their lives empty and decide to 'give Christianity a try'. Others are impressed by the words of friends.

And yet when you have found faith, whatever the external reasons may have been, you sense that none of them really explains why you believe.

This is particularly clear to us when we have come to faith in spite of motives which we later see were questionable or wrong. A family may decide to attend worship because 'it's good for the children to have some moral standards', or simply because their child attends the local church school. A person may keep up contact with the church because 'it's good for business'. Others find old age creeping up on them, are afraid of dying and hope to find some help in the church. Some people find themselves at church because 'it's the done thing' in the small community in which they live—and 'if you don't go, you miss out on all the gossip!'

God finds us first

We should not be too hard on people like that. Actually many of our motives for church attendance are quite selfish. But we come with all our doubtful motives and we hear the gospel being preached and receive Christ in holy communion. And gradually (or suddenly) the miracle happens; it dawns on us that the Lord accepts us and gives us a place in his kingdom despite all our wrong ideas. He finds us long before we find him!

Any person looking back afterwards will say, 'The fact that Christ speaks to me in the gospel and I have begun to trust him is a miracle. It was not my decision. It was God who led me to this point. I was "surprised by joy" (C S Lewis). Christ accepted me in spite of all my selfish motives. The Holy Spirit helped me to understand God's love and just trust him.'

God chooses us from all eternity

'In fact', a person like this might go on to say, 'long before I understood anything of God's love, God's heart was full of love for me. I did not find God. God found me.'

St Paul is found on his way to arrest Christians. Later he can only explain it by saying that God's choice had fallen on him long before he was born (Gal 1:15).

Why do I believe? Not because I move towards God, but because from all eternity God has chosen me. From all eternity God wanted me to share his life and love. God—Father, Son and Holy Spirit—has concentrated all his efforts of love on me since eternity 'began'.

That is the 'beautiful and glorious comfort' which Article XI of the *Formula of Concord* on *Eternal Foreknowledge and Divine Election* gives us:

> God was so deeply concerned about every individual Christian's conversion, righteousness, and salvation and so faithfully minded about it that 'even before the foundation of the world was laid' he held counsel and ordained 'according to his purpose' how he would bring me thereto and keep me therein. (p 624; see Eph 1:4,5; 2 Tim 1:9)

God's choice is decisive

God's saving, loving thoughts about us do not start when we commit ourselves to him. Long before we trust in God, he has been working towards us. God worked on our parents or on other people to make them our guides. Behind them stands the great 'cloud of witnesses' (Heb 12:1), the Christians who went before, reaching back to the first disciples and beyond them to the prophets and Abraham. Each of them was a piece of God's eternal plan to help *me* to believe. If I discover one day that the gospel is new and fresh it is not because I made a decision for Christ but because God put into effect a plan devised for me from all eternity.

Jesus says that in so many words: 'You did not choose me but I chose you' (John 15:16; see also John 6:44; 6:65). That is the gospel. My choice of God is not decisive; his eternal choice of me is.

Can we choose God?

People get alarmed when they hear that the choice is God's. Does God just walk into our lives even before we are baptised? Surely we have to make a free decision to trust God before he can help us? Doesn't our salvation depend on whether we choose to follow God's call or not?

Many people still think that God sent Jesus Christ to tell us about God; the rest is up to us. The view is that God cannot act in us until we have made a decision for him. There are still plenty of well-meaning but misguided Christians who tell us to 'open your life to Jesus' or 'make a decision to follow Jesus *now*', and remind us with a warning finger that 'the choice is up to you'. The Bible does not talk that way. But Psalm 65:4 says, 'Happy are those whom *you* choose . . .'!

Choosing—or waiting?

What is the use of challenging people to do what does not lie in their power? Because we are self-centred sinners we never choose God anyway, as Article II of the *Formula of Concord* reminded us (p 521). If the choice were up to me, who could blame me for feeling just a little proud at having decided to 'dedicate my life to the Lord'? Who could blame me for being fascinated at the way *my* life has changed since *I* chose Jesus to be my Saviour?

In short, if the choice is up to me, I no longer need to depend on God alone. I can depend on *my* choice, *my* holy feelings, *my* sincerity. The danger is that my eyes are turned away from God towards myself. And heaven help me then! For it is precisely when I think that my choice has brought me close to God that I am far from him. I do not love God with all my heart, for I am far too interested in all the 'pious' processes going on in myself. That is why we are really never free to 'make a decision for Christ'. Our decisions for him can far too easily end up in egoism. God has to decide for us first.

Do we then just sit back with folded hands waiting for God? We can certainly go where the gospel is being proclaimed, but then, yes, we must listen—and wait. And perhaps while we are waiting and listening we will hear what the writer of Lamentations says: 'The LORD is good to those who wait for him, to the soul that seeks him. It is good that one should wait quietly for the salvation of the LORD' (Lam 3:25,26). It is good to wait—although it may sometimes be agonising to do so—for those who wait for God to come to them will one day discover to their amazement that he has already come; their lives are already changed and their strength renewed (Isa 40:31). (Those who wait for God have already been found by him!)

The doctrine of election (or predestination, as it is sometimes called) tells us that God does not wait around while we are trying to make up our minds about him. While we are still wondering whether and how to choose him and thinking how complicated it all is, God has already made up his mind about us and done all the choosing necessary through Christ 'before we even existed, before we were able to have done any good' (p 623), before we could make a choice. And when that miracle gets through to us we have faith. Or as the *Formula of Concord* puts it:

> Our election to eternal life does not rest on our piety or virtue but *solely* on the merit of Christ and the gracious will of the Father. (p 628, emphasis mine)

God does everything

This is a great comfort. My future is taken out of my messy hands. God has my salvation in his sure, eternal hands. Luther summarises it bluntly in *The Bondage of the Will*: 'The mercy of God alone does everything, and . . . our will does nothing, but rather is passive' (*Luther's Works* 33,35). And doesn't Romans 10:20 say just that?

The miracle of grace is that God does not wait to see how we will 'shape up' in our faith and life. He chooses us from all eternity and decides in our favour in advance. The *Formula of Concord*, quoting Ephesians 1:5,6, makes a point of stressing that God

> saves us 'according to the purpose' of his will through sheer mercy in Christ without our merit and good works . . . It is therefore false and wrong when men teach that . . . there is also within us a cause of God's election on account of which God has elected us unto eternal life. For not only before we had done any good, but even before we were born . . . God elected us in Christ. (p 631)

No place for smug Christians

God does not choose us because we have faith. We have faith because God chooses us. Therefore Christians have no cause for smugness and superiority. Their faith is not 'theirs' at all; it is God's work in them. They have *been* chosen. The doctrine of God's election

> mightily substantiates the article that we are justified and saved without our works and merit, purely by grace and solely for Christ's sake. (p 623)

The pious, virtuous Christian has no advantage over the Christian whose life is an unholy mess but who dares to cling to Christ and trust in God's choice. In fact, that is the point of Jesus' parable of the Pharisee and the tax collector. Pious, virtuous Christians had better watch out that they do not depend on their sincerity and solid life but learn to trust God's mercy (Luke 18:9–14)!

An invitation to licence?

Many Christians have problems with this. What is the use of trying to live a good life if salvation does not depend on it? The *Formula of Concord* puts their argument this way:

> Since God has foreordained his elect to salvation . . . it will do me no harm if I live in all kinds of sin and vice without repentance, despise Word and sacraments, and do not concern myself with repentance, faith, prayer, and godliness. On the contrary, I shall and must be saved since God's foreknowledge must be carried out. (p 618)

Since God has chosen me—and nothing can alter that—can't I do as I please? And if I do make an effort and do good, it must be worth *something* to God? If I contribute two hundred dollars for home mission work or to fight AIDS, surely there must be something in it for me, they argue. Otherwise what is the point of doing it? God may choose me, but surely I have to do my bit too?

God's choice is all that counts

When will we learn not to think in terms of rewards? When will it finally get through to us that God's choice in Jesus Christ is all that counts?

And yet there are still vast numbers of Christians—dare I say Lutherans?—who think that because they attend worship most Sundays, say their prayers fairly often, concentrate especially hard during the confession of sins, suppress erotic thoughts about someone else's husband or wife, and water the neighbour's garden when they are away on holidays, they should be spared some illness or other, survive a car crash injury-free—and finally receive a special place of honour at God's side. Let us be quite clear: there is either the grace of God's choosing—or there are the good deeds which the law demands. There are no halfway measures.

Our thankful response

Why bother to do good, repent, be honest, kind, sincere, generous if God chooses us anyway in his grace in Jesus Christ? Out of sheer gratitude to God! Out of sheer thanks to God that our miserable little acts of goodness, with all their self-centred motives and our minute faith in him, have not influenced him in deciding to choose us and die for us. A child will often respond to great love and generosity by giving its heart. Anyone who takes the gospel of God's love seriously will make every effort to please God and live in tune with God, caring for others. 'We love because he first loved us' (1 John 4:19).

Besides, as the *Formula of Concord* points out, Christians 'should exercise themselves in all Christian virtues' and 'diligently seek to "confirm their call and election" ' so that they will not 'doubt their election' (p 628). If we refuse to put our election into practice 'in all godliness, modesty, temperance, patience, and brotherly love' (p 628), we will soon lose God's electing love. God does not choose us from all eternity for our private enjoyment. We are chosen in Christ to be 'little Christs', to witness and act (Eph 4:11–13), so that through us God's rule of love may extend to the whole world. Choosing is God's business; but we are to get on with ours.

Has God chosen me?

But if God chooses and I can do nothing, how can I know that he has really chosen me? Perhaps he has not done so? How can I be sure?

Wavering faith

Every Christian has the experience that faith has its ups and downs. Everything seems to be plain sailing, and we are happy, sensing God's nearness. Then we lose a loved one, or long-cherished plans are shattered, and we begin to doubt God's love. The nagging questions turn life sour. I don't always feel elected and full of faith and trust. I notice that my head is brimful of selfish thoughts, and I regularly let fly with my temper. Is that the way a chosen child of God acts? I go to church and feel nothing. The pastor seems to drone on, I don't *feel* sorry for my sins, the presence of Christ in holy communion doesn't move me, and my thoughts are too restless for me to pray. The singing irritates me, the fidgeting children distract me and I wonder, will the service never end? And afterwards I am full of critical thoughts about what the pastor said in the sermon. I don't want to be this way with these ups and downs, but that is the way I am. And if I talk to anyone about all this they look at me as if to say, 'Well, you've still got a long way to go, haven't you?'

In short, how can I be sure that God has elected me and that his promises apply to me, when my faith is so weak, wavering and uncertain? Perhaps God's loving will does not apply to me?

The *Formula of Concord* is aware that

> such thoughts may well come to pious hearts, too . . . especially when they see their own weakness and the example of such as did not persevere but fell away again. (p 618)

We are eternally in God's heart

The *Formula of Concord* answers our nagging questions by pointing out that the gospel of God's choosing grace is meant just for people like this! Our feelings or lack of feelings have absolutely nothing to do with God's choice. The classical New Testament passage which deals with God's choice (Eph 1:4–11) speaks only of what *he* has done! We are in God's loving thoughts long before we could experience him. The doctrine of predestination encourages me to see that my salvation does not rest on the strength of my faith at all, but on God's love. And those who dare to cling to that—whatever they may see or feel in themselves—*have* faith, and their election is certain.

Those who doubt whether they are chosen or not should listen closely to the *Formula of Concord*:

> God wanted to insure my salvation so firmly and certainly—for due to the weakness and wickedness of our flesh it could easily slip from our fingers, and through the deceit and power of the devil and the world it could easily be snatched or taken from our hands—that he ordained my salvation in his eternal purpose, which cannot fail or be overthrown. (p 624)

The doctrine of predestination is not given us to raise doubts in us. It is for those who already have doubts in order to give them certainty (p 618). Thank God our salvation does not depend on us.

Little faith, but a great Lord

Can we depend on God's love? Does he love us? The best guarantee for that is not our feelings or experiences or good solid life but Jesus Christ, in whom God's heart is open to us. Because of Jesus Christ I have been chosen. What God's attitude to us is he has revealed in Jesus Christ.

And what does *he* do? He calls ordinary people to be his disciples. Their faith is weak and wavering too. Throughout his ministry they misunderstand him (Mark 8:31–33; 9:32: 10:13–16;

10:35–45). When Peter most needs it, his faith lets him down—literally (Matt 14:28–31). The other disciples are no better (Matt 8:25,26). Even after their Lord has risen from death they will not believe it (Matt 28:17; Mark 16:13; John 20:25). Yet in all this Jesus shows himself constant and unwavering. 'Peter has only a little faith, but he has a great Lord' (Helmut Thielicke). And Jesus still goes to his cross to die for all people, including those who 'deserted him and fled' (Matt 26:56). That is the kind of God we have! He cares so much that he will not let our little faith get in the way of his eternal plan for us. He chooses us—because Jesus Christ made it possible.

God chooses us in Christ

That is why in its central statement Article XI of the *Formula of Concord* happily proclaims:

> We should accordingly consider God's eternal election in Christ, and not outside of or apart from Christ. (pp 626, 627)

That was aimed at Calvin, who said that in all eternity God had made a secret decision to choose some and refuse others. If Calvin were right, you could never be sure whether you belonged or not. Every doubt, every evil action could be a sign telling you that God has not chosen you. How terrible!

The *Formula of Concord* says that God has no secret plan for us which he has not shown us in Christ's life, death and resurrection.

To any who still worry whether God has chosen them or not we should say: Has Christ died for you? Does the support and help which Christ gave to weak and faithless disciples apply to you, who are just as weak and faithless? Yes? Then you *are* chosen! You *have* faith! Faith is simply looking to Jesus Christ for help, not to yourself!

God chooses us through the gospel

God's plan for us is not a secret with which he will surprise us at the end of time. It is open to us in the word of the Bible. And although we fail in our trust just when we need it most, that word tells us: God's heart continues to beat for you in spite of your failings, for he chose you from all eternity in Christ:

> We are not to investigate . . . predestination in the secret counsel of God, but it is to be looked for in his Word, where he has revealed it.

> The Word of God, however, leads us to Christ, who is 'the book of life'. This Christ calls all sinners to himself and promises them refreshment. (p 495; see also p 627)

Those who hear the gospel of God's love in Christ and dare, in spite of their weak faith and love and their obvious sins, to call on God for Christ's sake belong to God's elect.

The *Formula of Concord* therefore directs those who have doubts about their election to the word and the sacraments (pp 622,628,629) and to the promises given there. It does not direct them to their 'piety or virtue' (p 628). They are to listen only to Christ as he comes to them in word and sacrament (p 627), 'regardless of what they experience within themselves' (p 628). They can safely leave it up to the Holy Spirit to give them 'steadfastness and eternal life' (p 495; see also p 628). Obviously this means that we must attend services where the word is preached and the sacraments are given (p 629), and we must do this precisely at those times when we have doubts and whether we feel like it or not.

God's certain choice gives comfort

No wonder that the *Formula of Concord* makes a particular point of stressing the *comfort* of the doctrine of election:

> This doctrine will also give us the glorious comfort, in times of trial and affliction, that in his counsel before the foundation of the world God has determined and decreed that he will assist us in all our necessities, grant us patience, give us comfort, create hope, and bring everything to such an issue that we shall be saved. (p 624)

What more could you ask for? And isn't this the comfort St Paul gives in his magnificent Romans 8, when he writes that *nothing* 'will be able to separate us from the love of God in Christ Jesus our Lord' (Rom 8:39)? What God has chosen he does not let go of. What God has started he will finish. 'If we are faithless, he remains faithful—for he cannot deny himself' (2 Tim 2:13).

'None can pluck me from your hand'

Does this mean I cannot lose my election, no matter what I do? To be lost is certainly a possibility for some—but let's leave that to the next chapter. To be lost is, however, not a possibility for

> all poor, burdened, and heavy-laden sinners (p 631)

who

> feel that they are no longer experiencing any power whatever of the indwelling Spirit of God and say with David, 'I had said in my alarm, I am driven far from thy sight' (Ps 31:22), (p 628)

and who dare to cry out with their last shred of hope, 'Lord, have mercy!'.

Even if we consider ourselves or others hopeless cases, even if we feel we or others have let Christ down badly, even if we or others no longer know what we believe—and *yet* dare to reach out to Christ, we and those others can be sure *we are the elect*, the 'hopeless' cases whom God has decided to choose in love. And we can be certain that because *God chooses* us, 'no one can pluck us out of his hand', as the Formula of Concord puts it, repeatedly quoting John 10:28,29 (pp 496,617,624,631).

Loving Shepherd of your sheep,
keep your lamb, in safety keep;
nothing can your power withstand,
none can pluck me from your hand.

CHAPTER 16

Is God Choosy?

1.

A Reader: Your last chapter on the *Formula of Concord* dealt with predestination. Frankly, it left me up in the air.

The Writer: Perhaps you could explain what bothered you.

R: It concerns your whole approach—in other chapters as well. All you seem to be able to talk about is my private relationship with God. You seem to be saying: I can be sure that God has chosen me because of Jesus' life, death and resurrection, and so I've nothing more to worry about.

W: Thank you. You put that a lot better than I could have done.

R: But I do have something to worry about.

W: I don't see how.

R: What worries me is that you reduce the message of the Bible to a private, cosy relationship between God and me, as if no-one else were involved. You suggest that as long as I'm at peace with God . . .

W: You mean, 'as long as God is at peace with me . . .'!

R: All right, if it makes you happy. You suggest that as long as God is at peace with me, I can just forget about everything and everyone else . . .

W: Just a moment! I never said that!

R: But you certainly implied it. After all, if God has chosen me from all eternity, and 'no one can pluck me out of his hand', as Article XI of the *Formula of Concord* puts it (pp 496,617,624,631), then all that counts is that *I'm* OK, as far as God is concerned. You know, you go on and on, chapter after chapter, about the way some Christians are always looking at themselves and their private, cosy relationship with God—and then you end up doing just that yourself. '*I'm* all right, mate! He's chosen *me*.' That's what it all boils down to. It doesn't seem to matter very much whether I care about social and political injustice in the world. It doesn't matter so much that two-thirds of the world is undernourished or starving. It doesn't matter that most people today believe not in God but in Profit and in the inalienable right of all individuals to get what they want, regardless of the cost to others. If God is on my side from all eternity, it doesn't even matter that more and more people no longer have any contact with God. Because he's chosen me, *I'm* OK. I can sit back and enjoy my private relationship with him—selfishly. It seems to me that many people in the church are like that—Christian egoists—and their 'pious' selfishness is only fed by the kind of popular drivel you and preachers like you hand out.

W: You feel very strongly about this.

R: You bet I do!

W: Well, I don't think you are being quite fair to our pastors—or to me, for that matter. Let's look at the facts. Several chapters, including the last one, actually suggest the very opposite of what you accuse me of. If God has really chosen me from all eternity in Christ and is so concerned about me that he will not even let my wavering faith and messy Christian life get in his way, then in fact I have *no* more reason to concentrate selfishly on my private relationship with him. My life and future are in his hands, so I can stop worrying about them. As long as I trust him I can forget about myself. It's precisely when I realise in faith that God cared enough for me to die for me in Jesus Christ that all this talk about 'I', 'me' and 'my' comes to an end, and all the others he died for start coming into view. Even their physical needs become as important to me as their need for the gospel. At least, that is how I read Matthew 25:31–46. Although the *Formula of Concord* in Article XI wants first and foremost to comfort those who still have some doubts about whether God has chosen them or not, it makes no apologies for going on to say that

> Believers . . . should not be idle . . . but should exercise themselves in all Christian virtues, in all godliness, modesty, temperance, patience, and brotherly [and sisterly!] love. (p 628)

That is not a wishy-washy option (and hardly 'popular drivel', as you call it). It's a clear demand based on God's word. And because we are sinners and not just saints, we frequently need God's law preached to us to remind us not to be selfish.

R: I'm still not happy. You can't deny that this book generally has a very personal—I would say, private—tone about it. How do you justify that in the light of what you just said?

W: I don't deny that it has a 'personal' tone, although I would prefer to call it pastoral. The reason is that the *Formula of Concord* itself has this pastoral tone. Although it's a confession of the Lutheran church it doesn't just state bald doctrinal facts. It preaches the comfort of the gospel to the unsure and wavering as much as it teaches the theologians. It's initially concerned to show the individual, you, that God has accepted you and that you can rely on that.

R: That's exactly what I'm saying! The *Formula of Concord*—and so the Lutheran church—is really only interested in the individual's relationship with God. You just said so.

W: You're jumping to conclusions. I said the *Formula of Concord* is *initially* concerned with the individual's relationship with God. I didn't say it is only concerned with that.

R: I don't follow.

W: Let me put it this way: Do you get very upset when you read of some terrible car accident in your newspaper.

R: Sometimes, but not as a rule.

W: No, and as a rule it probably won't even affect your day's work and won't deter you from enjoying your steak and red wine at the bistro after work. For us a crash victim is usually just another statistic. For God that person was someone he created to be unique, to live with him in a sharing, trustful relationship.

What I'm trying to say is this: God's first concern is for individuals, and it is interesting to see how Jesus concentrated on individuals and how his help, healing, forgiveness and acceptance is directed to individuals. It is *this* woman, *this* man whom Jesus wants to draw into a living relationship with God. And so our preaching has to start with the individual too.

It seems to me that world renewal starts with the renewal of the individual. If you as an individual are uncertain and weak in your faith and you're not sure about the meaning of your life, you won't have much energy for anyone else besides yourself. If your house is full of darkness, you will need all the light you can get for yourself. Only when Jesus Christ fills your house with permanent light, only when you are bound up with him, can you 'let your light shine before others, so that they may see your good works and give glory to your Father in heaven' (Matt 5:16). There are no shortcuts to world renewal.

R: That was a bit woolly. Do you mean that the certainty of faith in God's permanent love is the only real basis for unselfish concern for others?

W: Yes, that's exactly what I mean. There are a lot more uncertain Christians out there than you might imagine. They put on a good front, but in fact many are more or less paralysed in their Christian faith because they're anxious about their future and uncertain that God really cares for them. And so they're paralysed in their Christian life and their concern for others too. They're much too busy trying to get some light into their own house. That's why we need to follow the *Formula of Concord*'s lead and help people like that discover God's breathtaking love first, before we can expect them to release energy for others.

2.

R: That brings me to the main problem I had with your last chapter. If I actually live in this close personal relationship with God and am certain that he chose me from all eternity simply because he said so and made it possible in Christ, then I don't have to worry about myself any longer. I think that's roughly what you said.

W: Yes, it is.

R: But then I *do* have to worry about others. Your last chapter left me up in the air because it said nothing about those who do not believe, as in fact I do. If God's eternal choice does not depend on what I do or feel, why are some chosen and some apparently not? The fact that God apparently chooses some and rejects others worries me most.

W: Are you thinking of anyone in particular? Or is this just an abstract, intellectual problem for you which really doesn't affect you directly?

R: What a ridiculous question! Of course it affects me. I mean, every day I meet people who don't believe. In fact, I often wonder whether under different conditions I might have been a real sceptic, or even an atheist.

W: That's hard to answer.

R: I know that, but it worries me all the same. I happen to have been born into a Christian family in a country in which the gospel is preached. That was by God's mercy, and, believe me, I'm grateful. But why was I put into this position by God and others apparently weren't? Other nations and races, for example. I could have been born in Iran or in Turkey, and then I suppose I'd be a Muslim and not a Christian. Just look at church history. Many generations died before the gospel ever reached them. And when it finally came, one town or village was reached and another missed out. In some cases the gospel came in a distorted way, and the result was superstition, not faith. Even in our western society many have never heard the gospel of God's acceptance in Christ clearly. It seems that God has withheld faith from some and given it to others. Think of the children who die unbaptised. Think of severely disabled people who can't grasp the gospel. Think of the people who have learnt nothing else than to get what you can out of life. I could go on. Can you blame me for being worried? It all seems so . . . selective. God seems like the football selectors before a big match. Some of the training squad make the team, the rest don't. It seems obvious that God has selected some and rejected others.

W: Does it?

R: Don't be obtuse, of course it's obvious! Doesn't the Bible say somewhere that 'whoever believes and is baptised will be saved; whoever does not believe will be condemned'?

W: Jesus did say that (Mark 16:16 TEV). But he was referring to those who have already heard the gospel preached. Above all, you should never forget that statements like this in the Bible are always meant to address *you*—who have heard the gospel. They're certainly not blanket statements covering those who haven't heard the message or haven't had a chance to hear it clearly. And you should remember that Jesus also said—to *you*, 'Go throughout the whole world and preach the gospel to the whole human race' (Mark 16:15).

R: What does that have to do with it?

W: Just this: it is certainly a terrible fact that some haven't heard God's call to repentance and reconciliation, even in our western world. But where does the fault lie? With God? Or with us so-called Christians who bluntly refuse to hear Christ's command, 'Go, preach'? The first thing is that God chooses us. But then we must hear God's royal command. At least part of the solution to your worries about others is to do something about it.

R: I take your point. I'd never seen the urgency of mission and evangelism in that light. But what about the fate of those people who through no fault of their own don't believe? Does God punish them because *we* have failed?

W: I wish I could answer your questions with the same clarity as you put them. But there aren't any clear answers here. Perhaps this is because God doesn't want us to sit back in an armchair disposing over the spiritual future of others. God's word is meant to speak to *us* and to show us *our* responsibility.

R: I'm not disposing of anybody. I'm merely worried about them.
W: Fine, in so far as they are *your* responsibility. But you don't need to worry about their future with God. That's ultimately God's affair.
R: That's not good enough.
W: Why not? Are you afraid that God's mercy is smaller than yours? That he's tougher on people than you are? That he loves the unbaptised children he created, the disabled, even the modern profit-worshipper less than you do? Is your God so small? Do you honestly think God will ever neglect a life he has created and condemn it through no fault of its own? But even now I'm going too far and beginning to say things I have no right to say. I'm not God. And as I tried to say in the last chapter: choosing is God's business and can be left safely up to him, 'for God is greater than our hearts' (1 John 3:20); and meanwhile you and I are to get on with *our* business for which we've been called and chosen.
R: You're really telling me to mind my own business, aren't you?
W: As far as saving and choosing or condemning is concerned, yes, I suppose I am. We have no business in the church playing God. That will only make Pharisees out of us.

3.

R: I've thought over what you said and have tried to read the Bible in the way you suggest, as applying to me rather than as a book of rules for evaluating the performance of others. But now I've struck another problem. What about my wife and children, and even my friends? Frankly, the last thing in the world I want to do is to sit in judgment on them, but as far as I can tell none of them show any interest in the gospel. They don't attend church and they're irritated when I raise the subject of trust in Christ.
W: That's a very common experience today.
R: Surely my wife and children have been entrusted to my care by God and are my responsibility in a special way. What makes it all the worse is that they've heard the gospel, and as far as I can see they reject it. They don't seem to want it or need it—as far as I can see (you're making me be very careful with the way I put things!). Does this mean that God has *not* chosen them from all eternity? Has he kept faith from them while he has given it to me? Sometimes when I think of my family I get very upset and I start to wonder whether God wants them at all.

W: I guess you can get very depressed when you think of your family's future with God. Most Christians face similar problems and ask the kinds of questions you have asked. And I'll make no bones about the fact that they are some of the most difficult questions in the Christian faith. For now you have come to the very central question of predestination. Perhaps we can work this through together. Luther and Calvin both struggled with your question. But it was Calvin who came up with the 'neat' answer. He said that in eternity God secretly decided beforehand what should happen to each person. Not all people are created with the same destiny. 'Eternal life is preordained for some, and eternal damnation for others' (*Institutes*, III,21:5). There's quite a bit more, but I think that's the gist of it.

R: But that's horrible! That makes God like a terrible monster, with us as puppets dancing on his string. That could mean that my wife and children may have been preordained to eternal damnation—and there's nothing I or anyone else could do about it.

W: Maybe. Worse still, you may have been preordained to eternal damnation.

R: Don't be funny! You forget that I believe.

W: Do you? All the time? Can you really say that?

R: But at least I try.

W: Trying doesn't get you into heaven. Only God's gracious choice does that!

R: Calvin leaves you up in the air, doesn't he? If you follow his view you could never be a hundred per cent sure of anything.

W: That is one of the reasons the *Formula of Concord* wisely included Article XI. The writers wanted to give Christians certainty. In fact, although the Reformed church no longer follows Calvin in every detail, this basic view has caused a great deal of discussion in Lutheran–Reformed dialogues over the years.

R: What does the *Formula of Concord* say?

W: For one thing, the *Formula of Concord* suggests that to hold this view really means to destroy the gospel of comfort and certainty. If what Calvin says is right, I could never be certain that the gospel applies to *me*. Every doubt, every sin could be a sign that I have not been chosen by God. I would have to live in constant fear of his judgment. Let me quote the *Formula of Concord*:

> Such a view, however, leads many to draw and formulate strange, dangerous, and pernicious opinions and causes and fortifies in people's minds either false

> security and impenitence or anxiety and despair. As a result they trouble themselves with burdensome doubts. (p 618)

People, being what they are, would begin to look around for signs that they have been elected—and others rejected. Churchgoing, for example, might be a sign that you have been elected, so to impress on other Christians that you belong to the elect, you would go to church. Failure to attend church regularly was sometimes interpreted as a sign that you were predestined to damnation, for otherwise you would *want* to go. In fact, some even thought that riches were blessings, given by God only to his elect. So if you could amass a private fortune, it was a sure sign that God was on your side! That was not Calvin's intention, but it happened.

R: Perhaps some of that kind of thinking is still with us in our church. We tend to make judgments about people in the church on the basis of their actions. For instance, those who attend worship are 'good' Christians and those who come rarely are not.

W: And as far as your family and friends are concerned, this might be a salutary reminder to you not to anticipate God's judgment too soon.

R: What else does the *Formula of Concord* say? I feel you haven't come to the main point yet.

W: As far as I can see, some of the older Reformed confessions deny that Christ died for *all* people. They claim that he died only for a portion of the human race, namely for those elected from all eternity. Now, you asked earlier whether God wants to accept *all*. The *Formula of Concord* makes a big point of stressing that we have to understand predestination—God's eternal choice—from the angle of the total message of the *gospel*. The gospel says there are *no* conditions under which God's mercy and love do not apply to me. The gospel is meant for all—for your wife and children too. And Christ died for them too. God is interested in the whole world, not just a part of it (John 3:16). He doesn't want anyone to be lost (2 Pet 3:9); he wants *all* to be saved (1 Tim 2:4). God's grace has appeared in Christ 'bringing salvation to *all*' (Titus 2:11). And in case there are still any doubts and we still want to put limitations on God's gospel, 1 John 2:2 adds: Christ is the atoning sacrifice for our sins, 'and not for ours only but also for the sins of the *whole* world'. Christ sends his messengers to '*all* nations' (Matt 28:19).

The *Formula of Concord* quotes texts like this with obvious delight (pp 495,620,621). When you consider God's will for us, those are the passages to start with. Luther spoke of two wills in God, a hidden one and a revealed one. The *Formula of Concord* won't even accept that! God doesn't contradict himself (p 622). He has only one will: love, salvation, the acceptance of all. And that is to be proclaimed in ringing words.

R: Hang on! You're getting carried away. Do you mean that eternal damnation isn't God's will for anyone at all?

W: Exactly! It would contradict the gospel to say, as Calvin did, that God is choosy. He's not. It may seem to be logical to say: If God chooses some he must reject others. But it's not scriptural. The Bible says to you and me: I have chosen *you*, and my love extends to *all* people. It would make nonsense out of Christ's cross to say he chooses only a select few and knocks back the rest. Why would Christ have to die for *all* people? So the *Formula of Concord*, in a very bold statement, says:

> Through Christ *the human race* has truly been redeemed and reconciled with God and . . . by his innocent obedience, suffering, and death Christ has earned for us 'the righteousness which avails before God' and eternal life. (p 619, emphasis mine)

Because of Christ's death and resurrection we belong to God!

R: I think you've lost me. You mean that this is the gospel and this is what we are to proclaim as God's will for *all* people? Am I to say to my wife and children: You belong to God; you *have been* reconciled with God; through Christ you *have been* redeemed?

W: Yes! *My* job is to say the gospel, live the gospel and to trust that the gospel will get through by the power of the Holy Spirit. And then I will have to pray and trust that God always uses his word to break down impenetrable walls, whether I see it happening or not.

R: It seems to me that you have come to a very different understanding of predestination from the traditional one.

W: True, although it is the *Formula of Concord* that comes to this understanding on the basis of God's word—and I guess you could call that 'traditional' by now!

R: In other words, predestination has nothing to do with God choosing some and rejecting others. Predestination means that I can know God has chosen *me* to share the benefits of Christ's death and resurrection.

W: Right! There is no predestination for salvation *and* for damnation, as Calvin thought. Predestination is identical with 'the eternal election of God' (p 494) and is not to be found 'in the secret counsel of God, but . . . in his Word, where he has revealed it' (p 495, see also pp 617–19,625).

R: But then the doctrine of predestination is simply another way of putting the gospel that God accepts the sinner.

W: I think you're getting the point. Predestination is to salvation only (Eph 1:4,5; Rom 8:28,29).

R: But I see that the *Formula of Concord* states that God's eternal election 'is concerned only with the pious children of God in whom he is well pleased' (p 495; see also p 617). I thought I was beginning to see light before, but this has me all confused.

W: Why?

R: Because it suggests again that God has chosen some special people ('the pious children of God') and hasn't chosen others who are not children of God.

W: You're being logical again! The *Formula of Concord* says here that predestination is to salvation only. It doesn't speak of the rejection or condemnation of others at all. I can't find a single passage in the Bible which speaks clearly of God choosing to damn anyone from all eternity.

R: What about Matthew 25:34,41? Or Romans 9?

W: Matthew 25:34 does say that Jesus will invite the 'sheep' to share in his kingdom, 'prepared for you from the foundation of the world'. But in verse 41 he does not speak of condemnation as prepared from the foundation of the world. The sects may like to talk that way; the Bible doesn't—not even in Romans 9, as the *Formula of Concord* shows (p 630). On the contrary, the whole point of Romans 9 – 11 is to stress God's *patience* with Israel (9:22; *Book of Concord*, p 629). The final word has not yet been spoken over Israel. Perhaps we should learn to appreciate God's patience more and show some patience ourselves with those who don't (seem to) respond to the gospel! In a way you could say: Predestination teaches us that God has prepared our salvation from all eternity but that the condemnation of some is still an open question.

4.

R: I'm still puzzled by one thing.

W: What's that?

R: Where does my family fit in here? I'm still worried about them. One thing is clear to me now: They have not been predestined to

damnation, so there's hope yet.
W: Indeed there is! God's loving will to save them still applies to them.
R: But what if they refuse his grace and promise? Doesn't this mean that they have not been chosen by God?
W: No, it means that they have refused the gift after it has been given. God has done everything possible to win them, but they have refused to respond. The gift *is* theirs; they *have been* accepted by God. But they don't want his gift. So if they really do refuse that gift—and we can't judge that!—then indeed they will be rejected and can only blame themselves, not God. God doesn't cause human opposition, even though he foresees it (pp 494,495,617). The source of opposition is

> man's own perverse will, which rejects or perverts the means and instrument of the Holy Spirit which God offers to him through the call. (p 623)

Or, as the *Formula of Concord* puts it later:

> The reason why all who hear the Word do not come to faith and therefore receive the greater damnation is not that God did not want them to be saved. It is their own fault because they heard the Word of God not to learn but only to despise, blaspheme, and ridicule it, and they resisted the Holy Spirit who wanted to work within them. (p 629)

Notice that the *Formula* speaks of active opposition, not merely doubts and questions!
R: That's cold comfort, I must say! If I believe, it's because God chose me. If I don't, it's my own fault. Am I supposed to say *that* to my wife and children?
W: No, you are not! These things are for mature Christians, not for beginners. Besides, your family is not yet judged. They have not yet been condemned. Not finally! God still allows them to live, and that's a sign of his merciful patience. Their apparent hardness of heart may be one stage in God's work of mercy (see Rom 11). You dare not be impatient in the face of such patience. You dare not anticipate his judgment!

Romans 12:19 ought to be written up where every Christian can see it. You can dare only to remind and warn—gently, please, not in self-righteous superiority! Above all, you can communicate the gospel to them as clearly and relevantly as you know how—speaking it to them, not preaching it at them! Through your actions as well as your words! By loving them as those entrusted to you by God, as well as by speaking to them of what the gospel means to you. For you haven't run the race yourself! You too are still struggling to reach the goal (Phil 4:12–14). A tragic event may show how fragile your own faith is. You could lose your salvation too.

But one thing I can tell you: God answers your prayers for the enlightening Holy Spirit (for yourself and for your family) with a decided yes. Always! That is what you are to do: trust *God*! Let me remind you again: It's not our business to say who will be saved and who won't. The Formula of Concord pointedly states this when it says:

> We are not, on the basis of our speculations, to make our own deductions, draw conclusions, or brood over it [the mystery of God's choice], but cling solely to his revealed Word . . . Without doubt God also knows and has determined for each person the time and hour of his call and conversion. But since he has not revealed this to us, we must obey his command and operate constantly with the Word, while we leave the time and hour to God (Acts 1:7). (p 625)

R: But the Bible does speak very definitely about judgment and damnation.

W: It certainly does—but not in order to get us to point fingers at others and make God's decisions for him. The *Formula of Concord* quotes Luke 13:23,24, where the disciples ask Jesus how many will be saved. Jesus virtually tells them to mind their own business. The question of judgment doesn't apply first and foremost to atheists and non-Christians but to *us*! *We* need to 'strive to enter through the narrow door'. Luke 13:1–5 makes the same point: Don't concern yourself with speculations on the fate of others; rather, take a good look at yourself! The trouble with us is that we always want to be able to sit in God's seat with a nice impartial view of what is going on in the world of the Spirit. Jesus has to remind us to concern ourselves with our own spiritual future. And that's a lifetime job!

R: Are you suggesting that in the end God will accept all and give them eternal life?

W: No, I'm not. Nor am I saying that in fact some will be cut off, locked out, condemned. *My* job is to preach the gospel, not to speculate about the human race in general.

R: Well, it sounds to me very much as though you were repressing the idea of damnation.

W: I don't seem to be getting through to you. Of course, damnation is a *possibility*, especially for me. But it's only God who can say: You are condemned. It's a future possibility which threatens me as much as anyone else. I do know that my own faith is full of unbelief ('I believe; help my unbelief!' Mark 9:24). How then can I condemn others? How do I know who has consciously decided against Christ? How do I know whether those who oppose God most openly, as the philosopher Nietzsche did, are not secretly searching for the true God? How do I know whether the freethinkers and humanists who openly oppose Christianity have ever heard the gospel clearly? How do I know that their unbelief is 'worse' than mine? Do I live my days consciously with God, trusting him 'more than anything else' (*Luther's Small Catechism*, first commandment, p 4)? What is *my* faith worth when I don't even keep the first commandment, the most important of them all? If I condemn their unbelief, mustn't I condemn my own? Maybe they will be condemned, I don't know. All I know is that God doesn't want to destroy, but for Christ's sake to forgive.

That is why the doctrine of predestination is not a lever for me to use in judgment on others. It's really meant only to comfort me and to help me see that I can rely on God's choice. The *Formula of Concord* quotes Luther to show that I can think about predestination only when I've already experienced God's mercy in Christ, when God's love has already got through to me (p 621,622). And it's worth noting that the *Formula of Concord* deals with this doctrine at the end, not the beginning, after everything else has been said (pp 495,496), just as in St Paul's Letter to the Romans predestination is dealt with only *after* our encounter with God has been dealt with. It has no theoretical statements to make about salvation or damnation in general. It speaks to you, to me, who somehow, incredibly, believe.

R: I wonder.

W: So do I. I'm full of wonder that God wants me anywhere near him.

CHAPTER 17

Our Lutheran Identity

It is often the case that parents of a teenager are amazed at what they have produced. The years before puberty are usually fairly harmonious. As a rule, parents can expect their child to cherish their own values or at least follow them. But one day the harmony is destroyed. They are faced with opposition, even open rebellion. The most unimportant question is an excuse for open warfare. Their most sacred beliefs and values are scorned. Many parents complain because their teenager has become a stranger in the home.

Search for identity

Wise parents realise that they are being confronted by psychological growing pains. Deep down teenagers may be loyal to their parents, even though they seem to oppose them at every turn. Actually, they are beginning to look for their own special identity and develop their own set of values. What is important in life we have to discover for ourselves; it cannot be imposed on us. Adolescents are trying to discover who they are, why they are here and how they relate to others. They experiment, they test, they compare. They try out new ideas, play with new experiences, and in the process they clash with the ideas and values of their elders. And yet if they are to discover their own identity they will need to take note of the experience of the past. Nobody can discover his or her identity by ignoring the wisdom and insights tested by time.

Usually, if parental guidance has been wisely balanced with freedom, teenage children will soon discover what is good in their parents' values and beliefs and learn to treasure this heritage. Because parents have had to struggle for their own identity they will know why they hold the values they have. People in our society cannot simply accept the traditions of the past unless they have discovered them for themselves.

On the other hand, many parents complain about the selfishness of their teenage children. As important as it is for adolescents to know who they are and where they fit in, their search for identity can be a very self-centred affair.

We cannot ignore tradition

Perhaps there is a lesson here for us Lutherans. We began this book with the search for our identity as Christians and Lutherans. Why are we Lutheran? What does it mean to be a Lutheran? Why is there a Lutheran church?

Obviously, if we claim to be Lutheran we should know why. There can be absolutely no justification for a denomination which does not really know what it stands for and thus has no identity. To perpetuate the divisions of the church merely for the sake of sentiment is irresponsible. It was certainly not mere sentiment which motivated the people who wrote the *Formula of Concord*. Therefore, if we are to discover our identity as Lutherans, we cannot simply ignore the wisdom and insights of those who came before us.

Making tradition our own

But it will not do either to speak in grand terms of the 'faith of our ancestors' or of 'our glorious heritage'. Like the teenager, we must struggle to understand what that heritage means for us today and make it our own, if we are to develop into mature Lutherans. The *Formula of Concord*, like the rest of the Lutheran confessional writings, has no real value if it merely perpetuates a position taken over four hundred years ago. If you bought your child a mountain bike, you would be extremely puzzled or even upset if the child put it away unused while insisting that it was the best bike on the market. You would want your child to take care of the bike—but certainly to use it. A bike is there to be ridden. So too a confession must be *confessed*, otherwise it is not worth the paper it is written on.

That is why our study of the *Formula of Concord* has aimed at helping us understand why we are Lutherans and what it means to be a Lutheran today. If we merely wanted to admire our heritage from a distance we would be better off without it.

Our God-given identity

Those who signed the *Formula of Concord* were prepared to 'appear with intrepid hearts before the judgment seat of Jesus Christ' and give an account of the confession they made, as they stated at the end of Article XII on *Other Factions and Sects* (p 636, see also p 500). They were confessing that their identity was God-given and that they were ready to stake their future with God on it.

Their words were not idly spoken. They call each Christian to the very heart of the Bible. They are a call to trust and to live in the comfort and the power of Jesus Christ alone! These people found their identity in the gospel of God's call and promise to all people in Christ. After many years of struggle they knew now who they were: self-centred, hopeless cases whom Jesus Christ had accepted and made God's children, people who knew that they had to see every aspect of life in the light of God's forgiveness and faithful kindness. And they wanted all those who came after them to discover that God-given identity too.

Self-centred identity

Of course, as with the teenager, the search for our identity as Christians and Lutherans can be very self-centred. We can be so concerned about the life of our own church, or even our own personal faith, that we selfishly disregard the faith and life of the 'one holy catholic and apostolic Church', which we regularly confess in the Nicene Creed—just as teenagers often disregard the life of the family they belong to.

The *Formula of Concord* was not handed down to us so that we would be selfishly concerned with our own unique identity. We are not here to build up Lutheran statistics, develop Lutheran structures and instil an exclusive pride in Lutheran traditions as such. We are here to fulfil a *function*. We are here to serve the task entrusted to us: to preach and live the gospel of God's grace to all people in Christ, along the lines confessed by the *Formula of Concord*.

A Lutheran identity?

Do we then have any Lutheran identity at all? Can we justify our existence as Lutherans—particularly at a time when more and more people are asking: What is the point of the existence of separate denominations? So what does it mean to be a Lutheran?

We have discovered that the *Formula of Concord* has really only one central message which is repeated in many variations: there are no conditions I can or must fulfil to gain God's approval. I have no abilities which qualify me to receive God's unconditional love and support for my life. The only 'condition' is that I am a sinner. Because of Jesus' life, death and resurrection God is on my side and accepts me as I am. So my life *is* good and nothing can really ever go wrong. And I can trust that! This is the doctrine of 'justification by faith' which the *Formula of Concord*, quoting the *Apology*, calls

> the chief article of the entire Christian doctrine . . . without which no poor conscience can have any abiding comfort or rightly understand the riches of the grace of Christ. (p 540)

To be Lutheran means to confess this and all it involves. To be Lutheran does not mean to confess some distinctive idea which originated with Luther or the Lutheran confessional writings. It means to confess the very centre of the gospel of Jesus Christ which has always applied to the church as a whole and still applies to every 'poor conscience', Lutheran or otherwise.

Committed to renewal

True, that central message had got lost when Luther came on to the scene. It was covered up by all kinds of other messages. Lutheranism began as a movement within the church as a whole. Its identity involved not a unique doctrine or organisation or structure. The Lutheran reformers simply wanted to call the whole church back to its centre in the gospel. The church was sick, and they wanted to heal it by reminding it of its one central task: to preach and live the gospel. Luther had no intention of forming a new church. His movement of renewal through the gospel saw itself as part of the catholic (= world-wide) church of the time. This movement was finally forced to organise itself as a separate church, but only after Luther and his followers were expelled from the church.

In a sense, the Lutheran church, although organised like any other, still retains the character of this movement of reform and renewal within the church as a whole. To be a Lutheran means to belong to this movement which exists like a thorn in the flesh of the world-wide church, reminding it that its main business is to preach and serve the central message of the gospel.

Committed to the centre of the gospel

When Lutherans state that they accept the *Formula of Concord*, they are saying that they confess the central message of the gospel of God's unconditional love in Jesus Christ, who accepts people because he loves them, not because they are holy or kind or good—or Lutheran. A Lutheran is a person who confesses that this gospel is central and everything else is peripheral. A Lutheran confesses the inner secret of God's word which *all* Christians need to confess: justification by faith.

So we have a particular duty as Lutherans. We must call the one church and the world to this centre. If we refuse to carry out this duty we have no right to bear the name of Lutheran. This applies not only to pastors and church leaders but also to laypeople. It should make us think about the time and energy we devote to our own structures. They do not exist for their own sake. They are to fulfil a function. If we fail to share our faith in Christ with others we may be a wonderful fellowship of religious-minded people, but we are not the church of Jesus Christ.

Joint Declaration on justification

Has the centrality of that message got through to other Christians? There has been a significant development in the ecumenical world on the threshold of the twenty-first century: the ratification and solemn confirmation of the official Lutheran–Roman Catholic *Joint Declaration on the Doctrine of Justification* at a special worship service on 31 October 1999 in Augsburg, Germany. In this document, which has been described by some as 'an ecumenical milestone' and by others as a 'backward step', the Lutheran World Federation and the Pontifical Council for Promoting Christian Unity of the Roman Catholic Church make the common declaration: 'Through Christ alone are we justified, when we receive this salvation in faith'. And the Annex to the 'Official Common Statement' puts it this way:

> By justification we are *unconditionally* brought into communion with God. This includes the promise of eternal life . . . The doctrine of justification is measure or touchstone for the Christian faith. No teaching may contradict this criterion. (Annex, paragraph 2E; paragraph 3; emphasis mine)

Is there finally agreement on 'the chief article of the entire Christian doctrine' (p 540, quoting the *Apology*) between Lutherans and Catholics? Is there 'a consensus in the basic truths', as this *Joint Declaration* claims?

Criticisms of the *Joint Declaration*

Some say the *Joint Declaration* merely reflects traditional Catholic views on God's grace which were already taught *before* the Reformation: God's grace, won for us on Christ's cross, is given to us sinners through the church's sacraments and renews us, so that we can stand before God as new people. We are made righteous first—that was the church's view before Luther came on the scene: God's grace transforms us and empowers us to love God and do God's will, so that he can accept us. Lutheran critics of the *Joint Declaration* say: That was precisely Luther's problem. He was utterly unable to discover God's love and grace in himself and so fell into despair. God, he concluded, had not imparted his grace to him. Between 1513 and 1518 Luther discovered that God accepts us *as we are*. We are not transformed into people capable of loving God. On the contrary, God sees that we constantly fail to give him the respect, love and trust due to him—but for Christ's sake God simply gives us his love and grace and acceptance *all the same*. God accepts us in spite of what we actually are.

In view of this teaching of the Lutheran church, critics of the *Joint Declaration* have pointed out (what the 'Annex' clearly states) that the Lutheran view of sin is and remains different from the Catholic view. According to Luther, we are and always remain sinners—but sinners who have been acquitted, accepted, justified. We receive God's acquittal, acceptance, justification not by becoming new people first but simply by *trusting* God and his declaration of love. Lutherans call this 'justification by faith alone'. And so we are *both* sinners *and* saints at once, not *either* sinners *or* saints, as traditional Catholic teaching claims. The critics have therefore stated that the Lutheran teaching on 'justification' is not just 'an indispensable criterion' for the teaching and life of the church, as the *Joint Declaration* claims, but the *only* criterion for what we say and do as Christians.

The *Joint Declaration*: a mutual confession

Certainly, differences remain here. But we should not underestimate the force of the *Joint Declaration* either. It states clearly:

> By grace alone, in *faith* in Christ's saving work *and not because of any merit on our part*, we are accepted by God . . . Through Christ alone are we

> justified, *when we receive this salvation in faith* . . . As sinners our new life is *solely* due to the forgiving and renewing mercy that God imparts as a gift and *we receive in faith*, and *never can merit in any way*. (*Joint Declaration*, paragraphs 15–17; emphases mine)

In a significant statement, Catholics and Lutherans confess jointly: nothing in a person that precedes or follows God's free gift of faith can be the basis of justification or earn it (paragraph 25). Only if we judge joint ecumenical statements by the principle 'All or nothing' will we fail to be impressed by these refreshing statements. And if we feel that the importance of our teaching on justification is not taken seriously enough, the *Joint Declaration* adds:

> The doctrine of justification . . . is more than just one part of Christian doctrine. It stands *in an essential relation* to all truths of faith . . . Catholics . . . do not deny the special function of the message of justification. (paragraph 18, compare Annex paragraph 3; emphasis mine)

It is a pity that the *Joint Declaration* is unable to spell all this out in greater detail—and that after thirty years of dialogue very little progress seems to have been made in understanding each other's view of the human being as sinner and justified. But the *Joint Declaration* is not a new *Formula of Concord*; it is not the goal but a milestone on the way. Catholics and Lutherans are not yet at the point where they can agree in every detail on the central teaching of the Christian faith. It is clear that there is a need for further dialogue. And both churches have clearly stated their intention to use the *Joint Declaration* as a 'basis for the continued rapprochement of the ecumenical partners'. The *Joint Declaration* nevertheless affirms that 'the mutual condemnations of former times do not apply to the Catholic and Lutheran doctrines of justification as they are presented in the *Joint Declaration*'. That is already a great deal. The document reveals that Catholics and Lutherans have come a long way in their understanding of one another and in their earnest desire to confess with one voice the teaching by which 'the church stands or falls'. Lutherans will be thankful for the 'consensus in the basic truths' that has been reached. Because that is what we are here for as Lutherans: to draw the attention of all people to the centre of the gospel.

The *Formula of Concord* of 1577 can provide the vision for us, for it is a model of what consensus *really* means: full agreement on the central message of the gospel.

Lutheranism or church unity?

But should we be involved in dialogue with other churches at all? Is ecumenical dialogue a necessity or a luxury? Some Lutherans still believe that faithfulness to the Lutheran teachings developed in the *Formula of Concord* exclude our concern for church unity. Lutherans have sometimes tended to live in grand isolation from other churches.

Throughout the world today most Christians, especially the laypeople, see the urgency of church unity. Younger people are turning to the Christian groups with the most attractive offers—whether these are Lutheran, Roman Catholic or charismatic. We have come to realise that our divisions are a stumbling block to many outside the church. The number of Christians in the world is declining, while some other religions are expanding aggressively. There are alternative religious offers on the world market. One may in fact ask: Isn't it *wrong* for us to concentrate on our identity as Lutherans, as we have apparently done in these chapters, when we should be thinking of our united identity as Christians? Is there a place for Lutheranism at all in today's world?

Formula for harmony

We dare not forget that the Lutheran Confessions are also documents of the *unity of the church*! We have been studying a document significantly called the *Formula of* ***Concord***, the formula for consensus, harmony, unity. The *Formula* was an attempt to bring about concord and consensus in the preaching of the one central message of the gospel. The writers realised that true fellowship and unity can come about only when we agree on the gospel. If there is no concord here, no amount of sentiment, no constitution, no organisation can bring it about.

But the writers of the *Formula of Concord* also state:

> We have a sincere delight in and deep love for true harmony and are cordially inclined and determined on our part to do everything in our power to further the same. (p 632)

There can be no doubt that the *Formula* was responsible for preventing total disunity among strict Lutherans and 'Philippists' in 1577. The confession seeks not to divide but to bind together. It is a product of the longing for peace and unity.

The main writers were very different personalities. It is said that Nicholas Selnecker intensely disliked Jacob Andreae. But their names appear one after the other under the *Formula* (pp 501,636). The gospel can unite even in the face of personal dislikes! The gospel was their basis, not their personal feelings. Perhaps we also need to recapture something of the genuine desire for true harmony with other churches—and perhaps be more tolerant of different faith styles within our own.

Committed to unity

Some may regard the Lutheran Confessions as statements of independence and separation. But that was certainly not their intention. As we saw, the central message of the gospel contained in the *Book of Concord* is not reserved for some privileged individuals or some specially advantaged denomination. It is meant for every human being without exception. God's will is that *all* should come to believe. The gospel of his love goes out to all. 'As all die in Adam, so *all* will be made alive in Christ' (1 Cor 15:22). If we believe this, as Lutherans we will be concerned for the whole world, the *oikumene*; we will be 'ecumenical'. We will be 'determined on our part to do everything in our power' to further harmony and unity based on 'the divine truth of the holy Gospel' (p 632).

We exist as Lutherans to point everyone to this centre of the gospel. We have a world-wide responsibility. This is why we cannot remain aloof. If we refuse to carry out this responsibility outside the boundaries of our own church we are being untrue to our identity. And we must keep our eyes open for indications of the gospel being preached in other churches and earnestly struggle with other churches to speak the gospel with them.

No unity without truth

At the same time, if we exist to proclaim the truth of the gospel, that truth is paramount. In other matters we can compromise, but never on the truth of the gospel. Does God accept me for Christ's sake, or is my sincerity and performance as a Christian decisive? Truth is vital here, because the gospel itself is at stake. The writers of the *Formula of Concord* show what love of the truth means:

> From our exposition friends and foes may clearly understand that we have no intention . . . to yield anything of the eternal and unchangeable truth of God for the sake of temporal peace, tranquillity, and outward harmony. Nor

> would such peace and harmony last, because it would be contrary to the truth and actually intended for its suppression. (p 632)

Some in the ecumenical movement have tried to bring about unity and harmony by avoiding the central issue of the gospel. Others have looked for formal unity as a basis for seeking the truth of the gospel. The Lutheran church has traditionally insisted that truth is the basis for unity. This does not mean that we must agree on everything. Nor does it mean that the voice of Lutheranism should not be heard within the ecumenical movement. But it does mean that for true unity with other churches we must agree on what the basic truth of the gospel is and how we are to preach it. To unite without that agreement would only cause confusion and hasten the decline of the 'one holy catholic and apostolic Church'. As the *Formula of Concord* puts it:

> We desire such harmony as will not violate God's honor, that will not detract anything from the divine truth of the holy Gospel, that will not give place to the smallest error but will lead the poor sinner to true and sincere repentance, raise him up through faith, strengthen him in his new obedience, and thus justify and save him for ever through the sole merit of Christ. (p 632)

The unity we seek

Those words are a program for ecumenical dialogue with other churches. And for that reason Lutherans throughout the world are earnestly engaged in the search for agreement, among themselves and with other churches. Our best contribution to the unity of the church will not be that we are indifferent to genuine differences, but that we find our own identity as Lutherans and say clearly (and humbly) what we believe. But we must also be ready to discover the same identity in other churches, even in churches with different traditions and different forms of thought and expression. All this will take place in a spirit of love and Christian tact. The *Formula of Concord* opposes false beliefs and does not mince words—but it attacks nobody by name. Where truth denies love, Christ is denied too.

Saying no!

But there are times when the church must say a clear no. The *Formula of Concord* still challenges us to take a stand when the truth is at stake, particularly against new movements and beliefs and philosophies which go against the centre of the gospel. The Formula makes this point by including Article XII, which speaks a clear no to 'other factions and sects'. The gospel unites, but it can also divide. It cannot tolerate statements or ideas or even lifestyles which are anti-gospel. One of the first 'errors which cannot be tolerated in the Church' is 'that our righteousness before God does not consist wholly in the unique merit of Christ, but in renewal and in our own pious behaviour' (p 498). We are 'practical atheists'. That is, in practice we make our decisions and go our ways apart from God. The gospel, the good news that God accepts us 'practical atheists' without any strings attached, cannot tolerate the law, which says God's judgment of us is influenced by our sincerity, piety or performance. That is incidentally a salutary reminder to us too, not just to the sects.

Responsibility for the gospel

Lutherans cannot avoid the responsibility of checking up on what is preached and said in the church and of determining whether it really is the gospel, or indeed something else.

Sometimes we will realise that by saying no we are adding to the divisions in the church—and that will hurt. Above all, we can only dare to draw boundaries between ourselves and another group or sect when we are entirely certain that what they say is no longer the gospel. There can be a certain variety in the presentation of the gospel which is justified—as long as the inner substance of the gospel of God's grace is not weakened. Differing emphases which do not affect the central message dare not divide. They may even enrich the church.

Taking a stand today

Perhaps the greatest heresy of our time is the popular statement 'God helps those who help themselves'. The gospel says no. God helps those who cannot help themselves! And he calls us to help just those people too.

On the other hand, there are dangerous signs, even in the Lutheran church, that faith in human powers of goodwill and love is beginning to replace the doctrine of justification. In spite of the overwhelming evidence on our television screens of the bestialities of which human beings are capable, it is still surprisingly popular to appeal to people's 'better' nature and speak optimistically of the 'little bit of good in each of us'. Here the church must say no, not merely to Mormons or Jehovah's Witnesses. People will hardly see the need for Christ and appreciate the gospel of God's love as long as they are convinced that the evil in us is nothing but an annoying deficiency, defect or disability in us—for which we are not responsible anyway—and that with the 'power of positive thinking' great things can be done and lasting changes wrought in our world.

Our identity

The Lutheran church exists to serve the gospel of God's grace in Christ. This is our identity and the one basic message of the *Formula of Concord*.

A great privilege has been entrusted to us Lutherans—but also a great responsibility: 'This is the doctrine, faith, and confession of all of us as we shall give account of it on the Last Day before the righteous judge, our Lord Jesus Christ' (p 500).

> May the almighty God and Father of our Lord Jesus Christ grant us the grace of his Holy Spirit that we may all be of one heart in him and constantly abide in this Christian and God-pleasing concord. Amen. (p 497)

References

Chapter 4

Helmut Thielicke, *How to Believe Again*, tr H G Anderson, Fortress Press, Philadelphia, 1972, 52.

Chapter 5

Keith Miller, *Habitation of Dragons*, Word Books, Waco, Texas, 1973, 71–73, abridged.

Edmund Schlink, *Theology of the Lutheran Confessions*, tr P F Koehneke and H J A Bouman, Muhlenberg Press, Philadelphia, 1961, 101.

Chapter 7

Gerardus van der Leeuw, *Die Bilanz des Christentums*, Zurich, 1947, quoted in *Christus hat viele Farben*, eds G Bezzenberger and W Erk, J F Steinkopf Verlag, Stuttgart, 1974, 15.

George W Forell, *Ethics of Decision*, Muhlenberg Press, Philadelphia, 1955, 153.

Chapter 9

Bo Giertz, *The Hammer of God*, tr C A Nelson, Augsburg Publishing House, Minneapolis, 1973.

Chapter 11

Schlink, 177.

'Leuenberger Kirchengemeinschaft: "Zur Lehre und Praxis des Abendmahls". Beratungsergebnis der 4. Vollversammlung der Leuenberger Kirchengemeinschaft, Vienna, 9 May 1994', *epd Dokumentation*, No. 25/94 (6 June 1994), 41,45, translation mine.

Chapter 12

Helmut Thielicke, *Christ and the Meaning of Life*, ed and tr J W Doberstein, Harper & Row, New York and Evanston, 1962, 33.

Chapter 13

Alexander Solzhenitsyn, *The First Circle*, tr Michael Guybon, Fontana Books, London, 1974.

Helmut Thielicke, *I Believe. The Christian's Creed,* tr J W Doberstein and H G Anderson, Fortress Press, Philadelphia, 1968, 127.

F H R Frank, *Theologie der Concordienformel, historisch-dogmatisch entwickelt und beleuchtet,* Vol III, Verlag Theodor Blaesing, Erlangen, 1863, 440, translation mine.

Hans-Martin Helbich, *Der Glaube im Kreuzverhör. Antworten für fragende Menschen unserer Zeit,* Christlicher Zeitschriftenverlag, Berlin, n.d., 39, translation mine.

Markus Jenny (ed), *Luthers geistliche Lieder und Kirchengesänge, Vollständige Neuedition in Ergänzung zu Band 35 der Weimarer Ausgabe,* Böhlau, Cologne, Vienna, 1985, 160–1, translation mine.

Jürgen Moltmann, 'He descended into hell . . .', *A New Look at the Apostles' Creed,* ed G Rein, Augsburg Publishing House, Minneapolis, 1969, 43.

Chapter 14

Eric W Gritsch and Robert W Jenson, *Lutheranism: The Theological Movement and Its Confessional Writings,* Fortress Press, Philadelphia, 203.

Chapter 15

Thielicke, *How to Believe Again,* 75.

Chapter 17

Joint Declaration on the Doctrine of Justification. Official Common Statement by the Lutheran World Federation and the Catholic Church. Annex to the Official Common Statement, Lutheran World Federation, Geneva, 1999.